LONG-DISTANCE
RUNNING:

CALMING THE MIND AND CREATING
THE CONDITIONS FOR HAPPINESS

The mind causes rebirth to beings
The mind causes release to beings
The mind confers victory to beings
In the struggle to attain the four
Goodness, Fullness, Fruition and Freedom . . . .
Sai Baba

SIGAMONEY MANICKA NAICKER

iUniverse LLC
Bloomington

**Long-Distance Running: Calming the Mind and
Creating the Conditions for Happiness**

iUniverse books may be ordered through booksellers or by contacting:

iUniverse LLC
1663 Liberty Drive
Bloomington, IN 47403
www.iuniverse.com
1-800-Authors (1-800-288-4677)

Because of the dynamic nature of the Internet, any web addresses or
links contained in this book may have changed since publication and
may no longer be valid. The views expressed in this work are solely those
of the author and do not necessarily reflect the views of the publisher,
and the publisher hereby disclaims any responsibility for them.

Any people depicted in stock imagery provided by Thinkstock are
models, and such images are being used for illustrative purposes only.
Certain stock imagery © Thinkstock.

ISBN: 978-1-4917-0834-7 (sc)
ISBN: 978-1-4917-0835-4 (ebk)

Library of Congress Control Number: 2013917056

Printed in the United States of America.

iUniverse rev. date: 09/19/2013

This book is dedicated to my Dearest Swami and my Dad Ponen

Munisamy Manicka Naicker, my working class hero.

Contents

Acknowledgements

I would like to thank my wife Allengary Naicker for her support. Thanks also to my children Veeran Naicker, Haren Naicker and Mira Naicker for giving me time to run and their support. A big thank you to David Schafer, Don Haripersad, Vincent Ciolli, Sagren and Vimla Naicker, Yaj and Varne, Mitchell and Indira, Pali and Kay, Runga and Marie, Jeff and Sharita, Sharmala and Nash. A big thank to my editor Veeran Naicker for his insightful comments and genius. Finally, thanks to the wonderful staff at iUniverse for their professionalism and commitment.

Introduction

The above quotation by Sai Baba is one of the most powerful liberating tools for human beings. The constant chatter in my mind and the manner in which it influenced my attitude and behaviour became very apparent when I noticed the difference between my silent mind after a long run and the constant chatter that took place in my non-running state. This realization was a turning point in my life. It became clear to me that calming the mind, learning about the mind and happiness was the most significant project for my personal growth and development. As a result the journey of reading about the mind and running became my most important and valuable pastimes over the last few years. I called it the Marathon of the Mind.

Arguably, the mind is one of the most elusive and complex parts of the human anatomy, and to claim any kind of expertise in this area is wishful thinking. This book is a humble contribution to the phenomenon of the mind that billions of people have struggled with for centuries. The above quotations at the beginning of this book suggested to me that we can change our lives if we change how we think. I know this is a cliché that is bandied about often. However, in making changes to our minds, we need to be conscious of what we think. It is a long and tedious process and personally, whilst I have made progress, I am beginning to realize that constant alertness of the mind is vital. It is a step by step process that can be likened to running a race. It is probably the longest marathon I will engage in.

The thoughts do subside after a run, reading a captivating book and watching a good movie but they emerge once one gets back to a non-running state. *The question that occurred to me was, how do I recapture the mind-set that I experienced during running whilst in a natural state?* I call this the free zone. I decided to make this my major focus through watching carefully what I think and intensely observing my thoughts. This was supplemented by intense reading of material on the mind over an 8 year period that also included running almost 13 000 kilometres. The realization that this is a long-term process dawns on me every-day and I intensify the process of watching my mind step by step. Negative thoughts and emotions as well as people you prefer not to think about, do surface from time to time. The secret is to persevere by not letting the negative stuff interfere with your emotions. This requires training of the mind each second, each day

The insights generated from the readings and focus on the mind has created a major transformation in my personal life. It is for this reason that I am writing this book to help myself and others to liberate their minds and live happier lives. I have gathered that whilst we seek happiness we live our lives contradicting that important goal. We desire so much, attach ourselves to the temporary and transient and allow our senses to dominate our lives. We tend to reproduce the past in the present but I have learnt it is possible to break this cycle.

Besides the challenge of the mind, the information and digital age together with consumerist culture places immense pressure on us. Consequently, we have such little peace and joy. A Lou Harris poll found that nearly nine out of ten Americans experience "high" levels of stress. A report from Indiana University says that one quarter of Americans have felt they were on the verge of a nervous breakdown. It is not surprising that the twenty top-selling drugs in the United States are for depression and anxiety. It does not have to be this way.

Training the mind and focussing internally is critical for success. The turning point can be reached if one is aware of one's thought patterns. It has to be a step by step process that focuses internally. Constant awareness of what one thinks is very important. The book talks generally about the human mind, memory and physical and spiritual composition of the human mind. It then attempts to provide a more realistic definition of happiness and suggests ways in which one can create that happiness. Attempting to understand happiness is also a major objective of this book and some views are presented on having a realistic sense of happiness.

The material world in the 21st century as well as the mind, memory and experiences is a recipe for confusion, struggle, lack of peace and constant mindlessness. It is clear that this information results in mindlessness and distractions. What will be the impact of the large volume of emails and text message on this generation? How is it impacting and how will it impact on the minds of people? The world we live in encourages negative desire, fear, pleasure and pain which are all ingredients of a chattering and restless mind. Due to our memory and our habits we all create little private worlds that have to relate to the private world of many other people. Our memories, habits and perceptions are often unique to ourselves. Being a social being, humans are therefore set up for confusion and struggles as our minds negotiate the hostile terrain of the universe in the workplace and the social world.

In negotiating the maze of life I think it is important to find peace. Stephen Levine in the book *A Year to Live* captures the reality of many people who were on their deathbed. He had this to say:

> many people, although they have few other complaints, experience certain remorse about having neglected spiritual growth, while even more express dismay that there has been so little authentic joy in their lives. All but those who have fully opened to life say that they would live differently if they had just one more year to live.

Eckhart Tolle in the Power of Now confirms Stephen Levine's view when he says that

> "Those who have not found their true wealth, which is the radiant joy of Being and the deep, unshakeable peace

that comes with it, are beggars, even if they have great material wealth. They are looking outside for scraps of pleasure or fulfilment, for validation, security, or love, while they have a treasure within that not only includes all things but is infinitely greater than anything the world can offer"

We continue with the chatter and the mindlessness in life until we realize that authentic joy is missing in our lives similar to the patients Stephen Levine talks about. As children we grow up with the fairy tales told to us in school and at home. Our school friends and siblings experience a joy that suddenly changes when we arrive in the adult world. The endless competition, tension and conflict absorb the best of us. The material world sets us up for a lifestyle that we could never imagine. This continues until we reach our last year's asking questions reminiscent on the inquiries into authentic joy from the patients in Stephen Levine's book.

One of the ways of achieving this authentic joy is through keeping fit, trying to understand the mind and creating the conditions for happiness. Happiness also requires some insight since we have to accept that life has both pain and pleasure. We have to embrace both pleasure and pain whilst we occupy our space as physical beings in the universe. *Life', as we quickly learn, does not resemble the stereotypical phrase, 'and they lived happily ever after.*

I remember sharing a conversation with a close relative in December 2005 when I said to him that I would prefer to live my life allowing my mind to be like a movie screen or not allow my mind to be influenced by my emotions or to be influenced by events everyday which is of a temporary or transient nature. The real challenge was to use running as a means to focus on the moment.

During my journey, which began with running, the most striking observation I have made was that we spend too much of time focussing on other people, their habits, gossip, and the impact they have on us. Another limitation is that we are consumed by thinking about the past and the future. The most productive personal intervention is to focus on the self. Once the self is understood to a greater extent, life becomes far more exciting. Self-introspection is key to our success and progress as human beings. Added to this is the focus on the moment. Right now are we enjoying the moment? Focussing on the moment involves a very serious attempt to not think about the future or the past. An enormous effort and mind training is required and It is what I term the Marathon of the Mind, which is a life-long marathon.

When we are in utter distress, the mind goes wild and the instincts take over. Where do the instincts come from? I talk later on about the sub-conscious in the section on memory. The distress is solved, as there is no other recourse that mind can take and the "focus" on the issue happens automatically. The challenge and what this book is about is to provide suggestions on how to subdue the mental activity in pursuit of a realistic happiness? Is there something called happiness? What is the human mind? Can we be more peaceful? What are the impediments to peace and tranquillity? These questions surfaced during my runs and reading of many books on the subject.

The mind is controlled in two ways according to Swami Maharishi; one is by thoroughly understanding the mind and the second way, one's prayer can make one's mind lose its grip and help achieve equipoise. Dandapani has an uplifting website which you could look at. He also makes a valuable contribution with regard to calming the mind and seeking enlightenment. He says:

"Imagine your awareness is a ball of light—As an exercise to see how this works let your mind focus your awareness on a particular thing (the finish of your last race)—that area of your mind lights up—when it lights up that area of your mind becomes conscious. "Using your will power and your consciousness you can take your awareness to any area of the mind you want to—and you can hold it there for a period of time. (My emphasis)

It is possible to create the conditions for happiness and peace through refocusing your mind in a disciplined and conscious manner. I point out in this book that the struggle for happiness and peace lies in exercising, understanding the mind, both the physical and spiritual component as well as the influence of memory. It is also important to understand the context of the 21st century. What kind of demands it makes on our lives? What is it about life in our current world that predisposes us to stress, anxiety, frustration and illness as a result. What is it about this life that sets us up for unhappiness? An attempt is made in this book to understand what is realistic when defining happiness and some practical solutions for obtaining a more peaceful state is suggested. However, there is a high level of discipline involved both at a physical and mental level. The biggest challenge that one will face is to keep persevering. As time proceeds, one experiences increasing amounts of peace and that initial progress motivates one to keep persevering. You will have the tough days, and the not so good days, but it's like a marathon, you got to keep going. Keep thinking positively. Your task is to think positively.

In my conversations with many people at various levels from executive management to other levels of employment, I found that people struggled with their minds. Many people, some of them who lead and manage large number of staff have at some stage visited psychologists for support and assistance. Others, struggle on in life independently without any help. A large percentage of the people I met and spoke to are not aware of their struggles in the little private world they have created through their minds. They believe what is contained in their heads is the absolute truth. People's private world impacts on many other lives and their own and as a result it is important that awareness is created about the mind. People in leadership positions, should create the conditions for harmony for there to be long-term and sustainable progress. It is very important that leaders make others believe in themselves so they can grow from strength to strength. When people believe in themselves and understand the value of creating a better society, they do not act as individuals. They act as a collective in the interests of the collective good of society. Human beings possess the gift of language and culture. Making the world a better place for everyone is key to the survival of society. Progress is defined by the value people attach to people in advancing humanity. To be mechanical is not to be human. Human beings should be caring, loving and considerate people who commit to the greater good of humanity. The easiest thing to do is what Hitler and other dictators did. They destroyed their opposition and survived on the basis of hatred and destruction. Hatred and destruction has never built any society. The Roman Empire, Hitler, Saddam Hussein and others have all perished. I speak later of living by the sword and dying by the sword.

PART I

The Marathon of Life is to tame the Mind

My running experiences over the last 8 years which included more than 13000 kilometres are a motivating factor for writing this book. The point of departure is that exercise and physical fitness has the potential to create the conditions for happiness when accompanied by a focus on the mind. Both physical fitness and an awareness of the mind are inextricably linked in pursuing a more peaceful life. Whether one is obese, poor, rich, consumes alcohol excessively, indulges in drugs or experiences a great deal of frustration in life, there is hope. During this period of time that I ran, I met many people who were not involved in any exercise regimen. Many of them got involved in running and I personally witnessed their transformation. The Marathon of the Mind is process and not an event. It requires conscious application each second, each day of our lives.

Having a realization of the power of the mind from a young age can lead to a very fruitful and fulfilling life. What became clear to me after running and extensive reading on the topic, there is hope for everybody in this world if you are single-minded, dedicated and committed to exercise which is combined with paying attention to the one's thinking. Each of us has a lot to do with what happens in our life, how healthy we are and how positive we remain amidst the challenges of the world. Therefore, I am very interested in attracting a younger audience since I believe they will have the most to gain from this book.

It is the contention of this book that many people do not realize that the number of stressful thoughts they experience on a daily basis can be subdued through exercise and an understanding of the mind. What this book emphasizes is that we have the potential to be happy, every-one of us.

The most important aspect of this book is that it suggests that the mind can also be applied to internal bliss. Bliss depends on how a person applies the mind. The mind has five senses which include touch, feel, see, hear and taste amidst all the external stimuli in this information age. The happiest mind is the mind that can control our senses, subdue our thoughts and develop a sound understanding of happiness.

My sense is that both psychologists and psychiatrists, although they are of enormous help to people, struggle themselves. I decided to share my experiences since I am of the opinion that it could impact on many lives. In this book I suggest that anyone can change their lives despite the complexities of the 21st century. This book makes a case that the secret of peace lies in the mind and fitness. It goes onto to discuss mindfulness which suggest that we should live in the now. An explanation of the human mind is provided making reference to both the physical and spiritual components as well as the role of memory and the sub-conscious in our lives.

Mindfulness is an essential starting point to peace

The *One-Minute Meditator, a website that helps with meditation,* explains the need for mindfulness in the quest for peace and happiness. They say that paying attention to what you're doing right now is mindfulness. Just breathing-that's mindfulness! Just walking-that's mindfulness! Just eating-that's mindfulness! In mindfulness is relaxation. How many moments of the gazillion in your life have you lived mindfully? The more you can count, the better you probably feel. They go on to say paying little attention to the present moment is mindlessness. Just regretting or fretting or wishing or expecting-that's mindlessness. Whilst in theory this sounds easy, in practice it takes a considerable period of time but it is possible. It requires of us to focus on each thought each second, each minute every day. Once we arrive at a stage in which our thoughts are being monitored by ourselves, we are making progress. The relevant question is what am I thinking now and why am I thinking this?

They argue that that stress comes from mindlessness. It comes from letting ourselves get swept away in an avalanche of thought and emotion. According to the One Minute Meditator, we may find many gems in that avalanche which include gems of wisdom, compassion, grace, creativity, and joy. We don't want to lose them. But we do want to dodge the hurtful stones of stressful thoughts that come whistling by at the same time. Unfortunately, the gems of wisdom come with a glut of other negative thoughts which can overwhelm one. The glut of thoughts is the challenge? How do we rupture those thoughts is the critical question?

The One Minute Meditator explains why this is so? An overly busy mind runs away from the present moment. It flashes between the future and the past. At one moment, you're busy regretting a spat with a friend. The next, you're fretting over blowing the toast at your brother's wedding. Absorbed in the past and future, one loses track of the here and now. And that is where stress arises: from missing the joy of the present moment, getting lost in the past and future. I speak later about the impact of the memory and the sub-conscious. We have deal with instincts and prompts that come from our socialisation into life. They could be childhood issues and turmoil that we may not remember but his buried in our sub-conscious. Those rear itself in our everyday life. The influence our thoughts impact on our responses to people. Much of the rationale behind our behaviour is not clearly known to us.

In the early days of my running, I did not know that the attempt to calm the mind is a life-long journey. As mentioned, this thought was motivated by the feelings I experienced after a run. It occurred to me that the effect of running was like reading a book or watching a movie. You have the ability to reduce significantly thoughts that consume your mind. However, the awareness or being alert to what the mind thinks must be a very conscious and on-gong activity. It is the senses that take the mind to various places. The senses could sweep one away at any time. An advert on the television or something tasty could refocus one's mind immediately. Therefore, alertness and constant attention of the mind is very critical.

There are 86,400 seconds in a day. The *One Minute Meditator* argues that there are about 3,600 per waking hour, or 60,000 thoughts per day. How does one subdue or not get emotionally attached to those thoughts? To not be emotionally attachment requires awareness of the thought and constant practice, practice by the second, practice by the minute and practice daily. After some time, a particular thought can just be observed rather than being angry or happy. After a while those thoughts does not affect one emotionally. Irrespective of what you hear, you will notice the thoughts and that is it. I have reached that stage with several of the thoughts that created anger or feelings of unhappiness. However, this is a long journey as I mentioned several times in this book.

It occurred to me that one could be happy at any one moment and suddenly feel sad. One could be thousands of kilometres away in a distant country but emotions of such as anger can emerge at any time about a particular incident in one's home country. This feeling of mood swings is a result of what one thinks at any point in time. *What you think is what you are.* My decision to write this book came about during the thoughts I experienced during evening runs, reading and peaceful moments of reflection, thoughts which I desired to share with others. I know that ordinary human beings such as myself, often struggle with what one thinks. My main focus is younger people who are starting out in life and who have a longer journey than I to travel in this universe. People experience a lot of pain and pleasure as a result of their thoughts. Many of my colleagues have shared with me their challenges of switching off from their daily tasks when they arrive at home. They also shared with me their deepest concerns and what troubles them. Some of these people occupy very senior positions in various companies including those in executive positions. They not only struggle with their work habits but also controlling negative thoughts that influence their lives.

According to the One-Minute Meditator, counting yourself as happy doesn't mean you enjoy a life free of stress. No matter whom you are, stress may get the better of you. As novelist/ essayist Virginia Woolf cited by the One Minute Meditator put it:

"My own brain is to me the most unaccountable of machinery-always buzzing, humming, soaring roaring diving, and then buried in the mud."

The website goes on to say that when our minds get carried away in this fashion, they can sweep us into states of stress and anxiety-even when nothing in our lives appears upsetting. One reason is that our minds work so fast. They pile up thoughts at such a rapid clip that they can knock us silly in seconds. The One-Minute Meditator cites scientist Mihaly Csikszentmihalyi who notes that our mind can process seven items at once-items such as sounds, odors, images, or emotions like joy or anger. If one reflects on one's experiences, there are times that a certain smell reminds one of childhood or a recent experience. How does that surface and where is that memory stored? Mihaly notes further that we need only 1/18 of a second to process each item. The result is that we can process 126 pieces of information every second. That's 7,560 per minute, half a million per hour! One has to start somewhere and at some time. Now is the time!

The One-Minute Meditator introduces a useful concept in terms of our unconscious. Our unconscious mind-out of sight but not, so to speak, out of mind-churns through information even faster, thousands of times faster. It is in the unconscious that we store habits of how to think, feel, and act. But we don't see the unconscious with more than dim awareness. Many of us do not have the ability to remember or recollect our childhood experiences. We do not have the capacity to remember hurt, insult, turmoil and other experiences that our sub-conscious churns out. Through psychologists and psychiatrists, we may have the ability to recall some of these experiences but absolute recall and a thorough understanding of the implications of experiences in our formative years is really not possible. It will influence how we think, feel, smell and act in our adulthood. We have to arrest those experiences that create unhappiness by being aware of it as soon as the thought surfaces. Having some awareness and control of our minds at the present moment becomes crucial for our happiness.

In Mexico and South Africa, violence and crime is rampant, similar to other countries in the world where there is abject poverty. South Africa experienced 350 years of colonialism and large numbers of the population lived in squalor. There was little nurturing of many children who were exposed to violence, drugs and other social dysfunctionalism. Many of these children did not have stable homes, parents and finished school at a very early age. They were brutalised by the system

9

of oppression. Other examples of this kind of development of children also happen in other parts of the world which include the poorer areas of the United States and the United Kingdom. Many social commentators enquire on why people become so violent in the press. Society is dumbfounded by the brutality of some of the crimes and the violence inflicted on the victims. Whilst we can never justify and defend violence, it is the brutality of their upbringing and the dehumanising of children that have made them perpetrate such violence. That is why we as a society should treat all children as our children. The world has too much of resources for so many people to suffer dehumanising conditions. The 21st century and future centuries deserves better but we need to come to terms with the reality of so many children in the world that suffer a very cruel fate. It has implications for all of us. In 2013 in the richest nation in the world, the United States, gun violence in Chicago reached record levels. As a society we must take stock of this reality since many of our children who experience violence become violent later. They pose a threat to a stable society. The section on memory and the sub-conscious adds more clarity to the issue of how children are socialised and how our minds could be influenced negatively.

We only see hints of our past life, our socialisation, in puns, jokes, slang, dreams, and slips of the tongue. We also see hints as we repeat behaviors throughout our adult lives that we learned in early childhood. Often we ask ourselves, why did we think that or say that? Why did we have feelings of warmth when we see someone or feelings of alienation or negativity when we meet certain people?

What is the human mind?

If one allows a problem to endure, it distorts the mind

J. Krishnamurthi

The human mind has the same general structures as the brains of other mammals according to Wikipedia. Sai Baba says that the human mind is a bundle of habits and memories. When thinking about the mind, many questions persist. Why are so many people troubled? Why do people worry so much? Why is there so much of violence in the world? What is the reason for psychologists being so busy? What is the reason for the struggle with the mind? Are we conscious of our thoughts? How does the unconscious rear itself in our daily lives? Why

11

do we reproduce our thoughts on a daily, weekly, monthly or yearly basis and how does the conscious and unconscious affect us? These are some of the thoughts that continuously occurred to me during and after a long run. I continuously enquired of myself, why many of the thoughts that troubled me during the day, disappeared after a period of about 5km or 30 minutes. What happens in the brain and what kind of chemicals are discharged in the brain that changed my thought patterns when running. Could I retain this positive mind-set?

I was at a conference in Doha in 2012 and decided to take time off spending a few hours on my own. During this time, I reflected very seriously analysing each thought of mine. My findings suggested that I focussed on three issues all the time which reproduced itself on a regular basis. This related to my job and how will I fund all my children in their education as well as the fear of the unknown. These thoughts kept resurfacing in a cyclical fashion and whatever I thought it was in some way related to these issues.

My reflections and readings suggested that the mind is made up of habits of thoughts and feelings, memories and desire. The mind is unlike any other part of the body. It can make you laugh, cry and want to dance at any at any time. It depends on what one thinks. It is the centre of behaviour as a person is influenced by the environment and one's own memory.

As mentioned earlier, the most important aspect of this book is that it suggests that the mind can also be applied to internal bliss. Bliss depends on how a person applies the mind. The mind has five senses which include touch, feel, see, hear and taste. The happiest mind is the mind that can control these senses. Training the mind and focussing internally is critical for success. The turning point can be reached if one is aware of one's thought patterns. It has to be a step by step process that focuses internally. Constant awareness of what one thinks is very important.

The mind is a reflection of oneself. What we see in the world is a projection of our conscious, unconscious, habits and memory that interacts with external stimuli. The section later on memory and the sub-conscious elucidates this point. We project a picture of the world based on our experiences, memories and habits. When encountering a new person or an old friend that encounter is deeply influenced by a number of factors which include our socialisation, memory, sub-conscious, habits, understandings of the external world and so on. There is little doubt that we see what we want to see based on how we use our past experiences. The world does not exist apart from each of us. If we do not think, what do we see? What we create we can destroy in our minds? Some fears and causes of unhappiness can be reduced significantly if we are conscious of what we think at any one point in time.

How your neighbour sees the world, how your child sees the world and how you see the world depends on each one's memories, habits, their sub-conscious, unconscious as well as experiences we encountered in life. We are products of individual histories.

If the mind extroverts and is controlled by the senses, for example, if there is constant desire for material things that a person sees but cannot obtain, there could be a great deal of frustration and anger. In the world today we are exposed to a glut of external stimuli in the media, on our cell phones and other forms of advertising. We are forced to think about what we see and hear. The question is can we purchase all what we are enticed with and how does this prevent us from silencing the mind? Almost all of us could be victims of our sub-conscious, memory and unconscious. The combination of memory, sub-conscious and unconscious together with the external stimuli that promote the material world is a very tough combination of factors that any human being has to deal with. Consider for a moment the number of people that commit suicide because of financial reasons. Living life is a long term project. Money could be made and lost and remade. There is no need to kill oneself because of a financial crisis. However, the pressure of society and the need to live up to the Jones's is the factor that destroys people. Therefore, in any crisis, it is important to have a long term view of it. In running, injuries are a constant threat but every runner will tell you there is a solution. Life has many problems but there are solutions for all of them.

If we live in moderation and develop control over our senses we are more likely to be happy. If we exert a lot of energy into focussing internally rather than being a victim of our senses, we are more likely to experience peace.

According to the One Minute Meditator, there is hope for everybody to see things differently, to think fresh thoughts and to move on from frustrating thoughts, people and situations. What we tend to do is to repeat old thoughts and actions. How many times do we repeat the previous day, week, year or decade in our thoughts and action? After meeting a friend that we have not seen in ten years, what do we think? What is our reaction? How does history shape how we feel about that person? How do old memories shape our engagement? How do old thoughts and memories as well as new experiences create perceptions of that person? It is important to allow the present to shape our thinking. The present is refreshing, it is in the now that one can alter negative experiences, thoughts and conclusions. The mind can control how you feel, think and act at any one time.

We always have the choice, every second, to use our minds differently, to be creative and move beyond frustrations. It depends on how much we want to turn our minds to the creative and new effort by focussing inwards.

In 2005, when I started running, my first half-marathon, one of worries was about finishing. I asked several questions of several runners about how they prepared and what did they do in preparation. My time in this race was 2 hours and 12 minutes. Subsequently, I finished countless half marathons and I never took more than two hours to complete it. However, memory and habits forces one to be nervous each time. The same applies to public speaking. Each event brings back memories, habits and challenges as if it is the first time one is speaking. Once again a lot of the pressure comes from focussing externally. The pressure of the race is really what other people will think. If one focusses internally, everything changes. There is no pressure!

Running marathons were no different. Before each race I had the same thoughts which plagued my preparation. Have I done enough? What happens if my muscles pack in? Will I be able to run up those hills? When I became a pacer for Puma and later Adidas, I asked the question, will I be able to pace as well as they want me to? The pressure always comes from the outside. When the mind turns inwards, there is no pressure.

My mind-set changes were more dominant during the marathons. I said to myself that I will alter my thinking and when each negative thought arose I replaced it with a positive one. When I set out to do the New York Marathon, I went to the start and said to myself that I will finish despite what challenges I have. This was my first marathon and my race only started at the 30km mark since I had done so many half marathons that 30kms did not trouble me. Millions of people lined the streets in the five boroughs but I did not see any of them when I reached the 37km mark. My body pained, my legs ached and my muscles were caving in, despite all my training. As the pain comes up it is like living in a different world, the world of survival. This did not deter me since my training involved visualisation and constant positive power thoughts. My mind during training was focussed on the passing the finishing tape. During the countless training sessions, I visualised seeing my brother Sagren, a generous and supportive brother, with a white beard at the finish. Of course Sagren was there with his family after making the trip down from New Jersey with his white beard and I finished the New York Marathon as Bruce Springsteen's song, 'Born to Run', blurred out loudly to my delight.

I applied the same principle to the London Marathon. Although I ran a half-marathon three weeks before the race and did not train for a month as a result of injuries, I visualised finishing. Two severe cramps on my calves at the 35km mark did not deter me. I visualised the finish during every training session. That manifested itself on race day. Each kilometre in the race engaged with a focussed mind that was bent on finishing despite the little pains and the negative thoughts. What happens if I get tired? What happens if a bomb goes off after the traumatic and terrible Boston Marathon incident? One step at a time over 42.2kms, I allowed my mind to free itself from negativity. When the severe cramps which I never experienced before set in, my mind controlled it for almost 10 kilometres.

The spectators and supporters on the side of the street do not help because it is about your mind and calming it. The motto at the start was I will finish and that is how it happened. The last ten kilometres was a walk and run depending on the severity of the pain I pushed myself and finished 20 minutes slower than the New York marathon. I never stopped till I finished. It was an incredible mental attitude.

I have found that we tend to think about 3 or 4 things on a continual basis every day as mentioned earlier regarding my Doha experience. We reproduce these thought patterns and they dominate our thinking and action. The challenge is to find a mantra or a sequence of words or word that can shift the pattern of thinking. Religious and spiritual interventions can help. You can remember the name of your God and repeat it when these thought patterns emerge in order to break them. One could be of any religion and invoke the name of Jesus, Allah, and Krishna or if you are an atheist you could invoke a mantra of a different sort. This process can take years probably more than a decade or longer to change the pattern of some thoughts and behaviours. It depends on how long one has been accustomed to worrying and thinking certain dominant thoughts and the determination to change. The quest for silence and quiet is critical in this transformation process. Sai

Baba says that the mind can run faster than light. According to Sai Baba, just as you are able to hear a broadcast of music from a radio station in Delhi simultaneously in Whitefield, the mind also operates like radio waves. Sai Baba says that

> Thought waves emanating from the mind have got also the properties of radio waves. There is no end to the waves arising from the ocean of the mind. Thoughts outlast the human body. Thought waves radiate very much like heat waves, radio waves and light waves. The thought waves are the cause of man's joy or sorrow, health, disease, birth or death. The potency of these waves has to be understood by man and his conduct has to be based on this awareness.

What is the role of Memory on our minds?

> **Perceptions, imagination, expectation, anticipation, illusion—all are based on memory. There are hardly any border lines between them. They just merge into each other**
>
> **—I am That**

This quote from 'I am That' reveals why Einstein indicated that he does not take himself seriously and why we should not take others seriously. Our perceptions of the world are a projection of the internalization of each of our experiences and socialisation. The socialisation and experiences influence how we think, react and act. Even in families, siblings appear to manifest different behaviours, levels of motivation and thinking. It is all about the different experiences we have encountered from our formative years that shape who and what we are. If our experiences involved many difficult experiences when we were young it manifests itself in different ways when we are adults. If there is a lot of negativity, we need to rupture that, change mind-sets and train the mind to deviate. It is all possible if there is a genuine commitment.

I mentioned earlier that human beings have a huge potential to change things, to think differently, to act differently and to live differently. I also mentioned that human minds are bundles of memories and habits. This shapes our daily life and we reproduce on a daily basis similar thought patterns and actions. The outer chaos is merely a reflection of my own inner disharmony. We tend to get disillusioned when things change around us or our views are not heard. We tend to suffer when we cannot adapt to changing circumstances because we do not understand that our thoughts are our own and it is on binding on ourselves.

Memory stands as an obstacle to the liberation of the mind. Of course memory is important, without memory we would struggle to make meaning and nothing would make sense. In fact we will not be able to predict our behaviours and most things would be unrecognizable. All our memories can be tracked to our subconscious and it can be called by our conscious at any time. Memory helps us to make sense of the world and our behaviours and responses are a result of experiences in the past. We are a product of our experiences and that shapes our memory.

New experiences, moving out of our comfort zones can be a very enriching exercise. It is similar to moving to a new country or taking a new job. Enormous growth can take place when change happens. If you are unhappy in life, it is important to change the conditions in which you currently operate or change your mind-set. We often don't have the luxury of changing our jobs or moving to a different place. Changing mind-sets is largely an option that many of us are forced to choose especially during this time of economic turmoil. Simply, one has to change how one thinks about life. Our taken for granted assumptions of the world will have to change.

As a young man I always wanted to change the way people think about race, class, education and other related issues. Whilst I think it is important to attempt to bring about an egalitarian society and fight the good fight, it is equally important to introspect and focus on one's own limitations. As a younger person I thought everything about the world was mainly wrong and I was fine. I have learnt that for the world to be a happier place for me to live in, I have to make the significant changes. I have to be happy! I have to see the good and be good. I am responsible for my mental health not the politicians, not anybody else. More people need to examine themselves rather than the world. In fact the world is a great place and we need to focus on what we think and who we are as well as what contribution can we make to make the world a better place. In this process we should not demonise others and diminish the value of what they think. We never walked their paths.

Memory is one of the important functions of the self and it records the impact of experience according to how it affects one. Why can we predict the responses of certain tennis players and politicians? We understand because we have been exposed to their repertoire of responses to particular situations. Psychiatrists and psychologists have done a lot of work on the unconscious with patients but are never really able to put their finger on how precisely the mind and memory works. Over the years and in some cases decades, there are patterns that develop in our personalities based on our unconscious and sub-conscious behaviours. People who are known to us can often understand and predict our responses to many situations. Personality tests are devised on the basis of indicating some deep rooted patterns in our behaviours for employment and other purposes. Often employers use these tests as basis to decide which candidate will fit into a particular job.

Our perception, thinking and general repertoire of behaviours and actions are shaped by our memory. Therefore, many people would suggest that human beings are a bundle of their memories.

Sandersen Beck developed a website and wrote extensively on spiritual matters and related topics. In 1987 he produced some very illuminating information on the mind. In view of his very accurate and useful work on memory, I have drawn extensively from the writings of Sandersen. I think most readers will establish that when they understand the finer points about memory, they will have to really make a special effort to silence their thoughts and spend more time reflecting on their own thoughts rather than responding to others. Sandersen's understandings suggest to us that we have so much of information stored in our unconscious or sub-conscious that it can make us very unhappy people, if we have a track record of many negative experiences with life. However, the potential for change is ever present if we understand the intricacies of memory. In the next few paragraphs I will attempt to explain Andersen's insightful and very valuable information on memory.

According to Sandersen,

> as soon as the experience makes a strong impression, consciousness is already processing, extending, and even altering the original impression. Yet these processes are original experiences making their impressions also. In other words, consciousness relates each impression to others in efforts to integrate the information.

I explained earlier that our thought processes are many and the mind works at an incredible pace. This means that we may or may not be aware of or understand the implications of what is being processed. Depending on one's level of education, intuition and intelligence, the consequences of this processing may have a range of implications. The point here is that this is a very complex process. That is why it is so important to be aware of our thoughts and what we are thinking. In some cases we could draw very wrong conclusions. Having an awareness that we could draw wrong conclusions is very useful for human relationships. Since many people are egoistic and want to impose their thoughts on conversations and in their work places, if they are aware that they could be drawing wrong conclusions, it will be very useful for everybody else.

Sandersen indicates that association is the process whereby consciousness compares aspects of the particular impressions to people, events, things, concepts, feelings, etc., all of which have been previously retained in the memory. These comparisons are based on similarities and differences regarding a multitude of characteristics. Therefore, the human mind is a very complex phenomenon and trying to understand it is an equally complex process. The process of training the mind, which is a huge challenge, could prove to be an easier task.

These associations Sandersen speaks of interconnect these memories, strengthening old ones that are recollected and providing new ones with a complex framework in connection with which they are likely to be recalled in the future. It is against this background that our responses, instincts and prompts of the mind will vary. Depending on who one is and where one grows up, the results of this association will be different. Think about the person that grows up in a ghetto in Chicago or in a South African township or a person who has graduated from Harvard University. They are all interpreting the information they receive differently. This explains why some people are more successful at universities and get good grades. Their history is compatible with the knowledge that is expected through social and cultural capital. On the other, hand people who have less exposure or are not socialised into to the demands of intellectual work will struggle. Regarding happiness, those who have been socialised into stable homes with warmth and nurturing are more prone to repeat that behaviour.

Retention is not a mindless, mechanical process suggests Sandersen. He says on the contrary, the consciousness is thinking and feeling and continuing to perceive during this process. So our history shapes our feelings and cognition.

We will retain and reproduce thinking that is formed as we grow. Social class differences and experiences become part of our consciousness. It is therefore important that we look at our past and establish what the gaps were in our lifestyle in relation to where we want to go to in life.

Memory is not just mental Sandersen adds, but emotional and physical as well. He argues that in fact, the depth, sensitivity, and relatedness of emotional and physical experiences are major factors in how well we remember anything. Furthermore, new situations not only remind us of previous cognitive activity but also of previous feelings and behaviours. This is a very important point. Studies have revealed that most people in prisons across the world had some kind of abuse in childhood. What we experience when we are young has a number of implications for us when we are adults. However, one does not have to be poor to have emotional and other scars. All people, rich and poor, have these emotional scars. For example, divorce often has challenging impact on children when they become adults. The relationship between any couple affects and impacts on the development of their offspring. Changing our mind-sets becomes crucial for our liberation. Our shift to focus on the present and enjoy the moment is possible but if we consider our memories we should be forced to act quickly on this point. Alternatively, we will relive the past on an everyday basis. The child from Chicago or the child born in a slum in Bangaladesh can change their circumstances. It is for this reason that I added a substantial section on supporting children who struggle in this book. People who are exposed to trauma and disadvantaged have real scars and it is this emotional overload that often prevents them from living a fulfilling life.

The memorized behaviour patterns of the mind, emotions, and physical body have been called habits according to Sandersen. This is a very significant point since many of us have scripted habits based on how we were socialised. Someone who has been exposed to alcoholic, gambling and undisciplined adults will inculcate these habits. Sandersen points out further that habit can be distinguished from autonomic responses, which are basically reflexes. Habits are formed by a combination of instinctive needs, subconscious tendencies, and the originally conscious choices of learning and training which with repetition soon become subconscious. The repetition and training in our subconscious is the most challenging to change. It is likely that if we are not aware of these habits we will reproduce it until we leave this earth. Alternatively, if we are conscious of our thought processes, and make a determined attempt to change, change is possible. According to Sandersen, the body "remembers" how to behave in similar situations. Therefore, our instincts and responses as adults are shaped in our early years. The more confident we are or our levels of insecurities in adult lives come from the early years. Children in homes that are stable behave differently from homes that are unstable. Therefore it is important for us to train our minds to free ourselves if we experience a greater degree of frustration or if we experienced trauma in our early years.

What takes place in early learning is most significant. The earlier the learning and the consistency of the learning creates the possibility for habits to develop which is later entrenched in our repertoire of behaviours. Hopefully, our habits are good but in general many people struggle with habits that are formed very early in life that affect them negatively. Thinking negatively, fear and different phobias are some examples. In similar ways the child from the Chicago ghetto who has been exposed to violence and crime has certain learned behaviours. We all have learnt behaviours. Virtually all of us have a repertoire of behaviours that influence how we respond to situations. If they are negative, we CAN change it. It is very important to know that whatever is constructed by the mind can be deconstructed.

Dogs and circus animals can be trained to do almost anything you want them to do. Psychological experiments have shown on several occasions the power of training and conditioning. Sandersen remarks that training and conditioning can develop these habits, because our physical system is able to remember from past experience what to do and how to make specific adjustments for the variations of each situation. Human beings have the ability and insight to change. However, this is not possible if one does not rupture the thought patterns. A clear point of departure here will be to observe what one thinks in order to change. Training the mind once again becomes crucial to undo training and conditioning. Conscious attention is used to form a habit or to change an old habit to a new pattern. That is the greatest advice anybody can take from this book. We can change our habits. We as adults or young adults cannot blame our past. Where we grow up and with whom we grow up really do not matter if we consciously want to change our habits.

Having insight into ones behaviour is very important. If we could learn this as a subject in school, it will help many people live a far more fulfilling life. Imagine if children in the from a Chicago ghetto, in South African slums and in the Brazilian favela's learnt at school about behaviour and how the environment affects one. Can you imagine if there was a subject at school that helped children understands how the mind shapes behaviour and the implications of memory on the mind, habits and desires? Surely, we could decrease the unhappiness and have people lead more holistic lives.

Can you imagine if teachers and educationists responsible for children in the Chicago ghetto, South African slums and in the Favelas in Brazil all understand the effect of social experiences, memory and habits of these children when developing policy on education and implementation strategies? They will first attempt to undo the damage in the formative years and the curriculum shaping process will be central to this. The curriculum in schools cannot be a mechanical concept that is divorced from the lived reality of large numbers of children who experience so much of trauma which becomes a part of their consciousness.

Changing conditioned responses can be a struggle, because the mind, brain, and cells of the body must remember to perform the new response over the previous memories of the old, thus the special need for conscious effort according to Sandersen. The need to rupture old patterns will prove to be a challenge given the manner in which certain habits and desires have been internalized. Focussing on the moment and reshaping one's live could make a big difference. Ultimately, the tools for change exist but it has to be accompanied by a deep desire to change. We should think about exposing children who live in difficult circumstances to knowledge that can liberate them particularly those children who live in difficult circumstances.

According to Sanderson, for a while the two responses may rival each other; when the new conscious purpose relaxes, the old habit pattern may slip in during familiar circumstances. That is why it is important to be aware of one's thoughts each second, each minute and each day. These subconscious memories and behavioural habits are held and performed by the basic self. The conscious self is responsible for the training of the basic self and the conscious choices of retraining. For younger people, given the huge challenge and the possibility of being swept away the by endless stream of thoughts, intervention at a systemic level, for example, at school can make a huge difference. Meditation and silence should become part of the school day.

What this all means is that we will have to clear our minds and leave the baggage behind. You would have gathered by now that this is not an easy task. Given the years of repetitive thoughts, action and behaviour, it is indeed a challenge but there is sufficient evidence that changes can take place. A good example is the effectiveness of rehabilitation but for rehabilitation to be effective, conducive environments are essential. In the case of individuals who have the inner strength to change and embark on a new life, it is the mind that they need to focus on. They can do it themselves in any environment because their minds are the tools for liberation not anything else.

The spiritualists suggest that we have to embrace the greater good of the world and see oneself as part of the world. We have to trust in the greater good. Step away from the ego and trust in the universe. If the mind extroverts its senses, it becomes the reason for bondage says Sai Baba. By the inspiration of the intellect if the mind introverts to seek happiness then it becomes an instrument to liberate itself. Spirituality is a useful tool to obtain support for change. There are about seven billion people in the world most of whom struggle on a daily basis. Spirituality seems to be our only solution as Stephen Levine reminds us about his patients and the need for authentic joy.

In recent times, I have tried to break out of the shackles of my memory by pushing myself to do things differently. I have attempted to see people differently and not judge them based on my own mind-set. I have focussed less on the faults of others but rather on my own responses to people. Further, I have tended to judge less given the impact of people's histories on their lives. There has been a realization that what is in my head is not necessarily the truth and the same applies to all other people. Fortunately, I am more forgiving and understanding since I realize that people in general and myself are not perfect. An important realization for me is that what conclusions I have drawn only apply to me. It does not apply to anybody else.

My attitude to this change is that there has to be an emphasis on imagination. 80 percent imagination and 20% memory has become my new motto. In other words I have tried not to rely on memory too much, despite the difficulty associated with this, and focus on imagination. This is the emergence of a new destiny for me. Whilst I spend much of my time noting what I think and carefully tracking my thoughts, I have also placed emphasis on using my imagination and visualizing a different happier space. Whilst this has been a long journey the fruits are beginning to emerge. A break with past and a venture into a new positive space.

I am also trying to see myself as part of a broader universe. A universe that is a kind one and that my destiny lies in the hands of a Divine Being or a Supreme Being. There is nothing that I do today which I can claim with confidence that I have achieved on my own. A similar thing could be said for many other people as much as we would like to claim the progress we made is of our own doing. There is a broader consciousness that we all have to subscribe to and be subject to the will of the universe. If one treats the universe kindly there is a reciprocal response. I believe that if one causes harm to the universe there is a similar response. More practically we are here to assist and support others in reaching their goals.

Some spiritual dimensions of the Mind

The world is indeed a mysterious place. Whilst history, sociology and science help to explain phenomena, a lot of what happens in the world falls into the metaphysical realm. Why do certain people die young? Why do we meet certain people? Why do we marry someone? Why is that we have certain friends? Why are we closer to some and not others? Why do we develop a preference for certain things? The list and the questions are endless.

The mind, memory and the subconscious are complex. Spiritual aspirants have devoted thousands of years devoting their time to the divine. I thought that this is really something that should be injected into the debate about the mind. Whilst human beings struggle to calm and control their thoughts, sages and spiritual aspirants over the ages have achieved a considerable amount of success. It is for this reason that I thought it useful to draw on some of this wisdom which is absolutely essential in the 21st century. Remember at the very beginning of this book, we were reminded by Stephen Levine that people sought authentic joy when they were told they had a year to live. Spirituality promises that joy more than anything else in life since it can become a permanent feature without living like hermits in a forest. A lot of what exists in the material world is temporary and transient. The spiritual world offers very permanent internal joy which is endless. I want to refer you once again to the powerful quote by Tolle at the beginning of this book. He says that our wealth lies within us and that is spiritual wealth.

Luchrmann picked up the debate in the New York Times recently on the politics of belief or faith. He argues that people do not want to get involved in this debate. He says what he saw after his years of spending time in evangelical churches, that people went to church to experience joy and to learn how to have more of it. Further, Luchrmann points out that

> these days he finds that it is more helpful to think about faith as the questions people choose to focus on, rather than the propositions observers think they must hold. "If you can sidestep the problem of belief—and the related politics, which can be so distracting—it is easier to see that the evangelical view of the world is full of joy. God is good. The world is good. Things will be good, even if they don't seem good now. That's what draws people to church. It is understandably hard for secular observers to sidestep the problem of belief. But it is worth appreciating that in belief is the reach for joy, and the reason many people go to church in the first place"

The mind of people has to have a focus. The focus on the divine and joy will help many people to survive struggle and challenges.

There were several responses to this debate about faith and belief in Luchrmann article. The first response was from a physician. He had this to say:

"As a physician, it is easy to identify someone who is spiritual—when I enter the room; they are serene and are upbeat. When I then confirm with them that they are spiritual, I then share with them a story of a personal connection that another person had with God. When asked if they have had that connection, half of the time these individuals have had very specific experiences, such as a voice speaking to them that allowed them to avert tragedy at the last minute, which was a defining moment in their lives; subsequently, they become more intuitive and 'connected'. These are private experiences they have often not shared with others. And these are in grounded individuals. I have learned that for very, very many, it is these personal encounters that lead to irrevocable belief and comfort in God—it is not abstract for them. This is very similar to my many patients with near death experiences. They no longer have any doubts as to their spiritual connections; what they experienced was more real than reality, and they no longer have fear. Living life without fear is transforming.

The second comment in the New York Times article went like this:

While the sentiment, "God is good. The world is good. Things will be good, even if they don't seem good now. That's what draws people to church," is charming, it overlooks the fact that for many their deity seems at best indifferent, if not downright hostile, and that the world not only does not seem good, but in fact, offers no promise for the future.

If one analyses both comments it seems there are two positions on this matter. The first being the believer and the second a person frustrated with what is going on in this beautiful universe. My view on this matter is that there are so many issues and complexities in the world that should be changed. This is impossible in our lifetime. A more pragmatic approach will be to change oneself and see the good in the world. Once one sees the good, one can work from a position of strength to make changes.

Given what we hear in the press and the media, it is very easy for people to become discouraged by the world. Further, there are people like the one who made the latter comment to the New York Times article that suggests that person will remain with a hostile position which will impact on the person's well-being. People tend to become more cynical as they experience the world. However, in the Dialogues of Sr Nisargadatta Maharaj in 'I am That', he says that

> Happiness is incidental. The true and effective motive is love. You see people suffer and you seek the best way of helping them. The answer is obvious—first put yourself beyond the need of help. Be sure your attitude is of pure goodwill, free of expectation of any kind (cause of unhappiness). Those who seek mere happiness may end up in sublime indifference, while love will never rest.

The real challenge is for people to change themselves and operate from the basis of love. It is important to draw from spiritual sources to increase our knowledge base instead of rejecting information based on the fact that one does not believe. For this reason I attempt to provide useful insights I gleaned from the Summer Showers talks given by Sai Baba in 1990. In these talks Sai Baba was talking to students in India. I am quite convinced that listening to these talks will assist many people irrespective of their faith. Sai Baba has spoken extensively on the mind and has generated several ideas on the issue of the mind and related matters.

He says that the Soul has three powers associated with it. Firstly, the mind has a vastness that cannot be described. He says that it can travel any distance in a trice and has power beyond description and human comprehension. Even a small task cannot be accomplished without the power of the mind which has no form. It derives its power from the Soul. Therefore, it is the Inner Self that operates through the mind and performs all activities in the world. He says that ages of effort are inadequate to understand the nature of the mind. Therefore, it is crucial that we use the mind to liberate us rather than oppress us. The language of liberation is shaped by positive thinking.

In the case of the two comments in the New York times mentioned earlier, who do you think will be happier, the one who sees the world as good or the person who sees the world as hostile? Using positive thinking as a point of departure will have enormous benefit for the individual and society at large. After a Tsunami or tornado, who are the people that are most constructive? Are they those that lie back and see the worst of the disaster or those who offer to help? Reflecting on television coverage of these events, despite the devastation, the happiest people are those who go out and help. The secret is to have a positive attitude irrespective of what happens. Those people will ultimately be the survivors. I mention in this book Victor Frankl who spoke about his experiences in the holocaust. If he didn't? use his mind positively and constructively, he would have never survived. He most probably would have committed suicide.

Secondly, the intellect is full of illumination and has the ability to discriminate between good and evil without giving room to selfishness. Therefore, in every situation we have a choice. The choice to discriminate between good and bad is often obvious. Thirdly, its results are experienced not only in the present birth but in the future births also. Man is required to give up wickedness and cultivate goodness in thought word and deed.

Sai Baba says that the scripture declares that the cosmos is made up of thought waves. The mind is the root of the cosmos and there is no place or form or action wherein the mind is absent. Hence, all thoughts of man should be turned in the right direction. Sai Baba goes on to say that whoever wields the sword against others, will perish by the sword . . . As are the thoughts, so is the outcome. The entire human existence is based upon thoughts and their results.

If we revert back to the Roman Empire, it becomes clear that the fall of the empire can best be captured by the saying that those who live by the sword perish by the sword. Another very good example was that of apartheid South Africa. Generations of people in the past made it very difficult for their children and grandchildren who were the oppressors. They made their children believe in an ideology that was false. Fortunately, Nelson Mandela had the wisdom to create the conditions of harmony which saved South Africa from turmoil.

Sai Baba adds further that man commits many offences, knowingly or unknowingly, not only in this life but also in previous lives. The imprint of these actions is carried by the memory, life after life, like dust accumulating on the surface of a mirror day after day. Thus, the mirror of man's mind gets covered up by such dirt, which is technically named as "mala". On account of this mala, man is unable to see clearly the reflection of his real identity in the mirror of his mind. Hence, it is necessary to cleanse the mirror of the impurities covering it. This cleansing is done by regulating one's food and other living habits, including recreation. He advises that students particularly should strictly avoid eating impure food. Purity should be ensured with regard to the vessels used for cooking the food materials used for cooking, and thirdly, the process of cooking. In this connection, an important point which is generally overlooked is the fact that many of the ills from which people suffer today are due to consuming things obtained through unfair means as well as polluted by the bad vibrations from cooks of questionable character. It is extremely difficult, if not altogether impossible, especially in the present day context, to ensure such purity in all these respects and at all times.

Sai Baba advises that to get over these practical difficulties, the way out suggested by the scriptures is to offer the food to God before eating it, duly regarding it as God's gift. I am aware that Christians do a prayer of thanks before they eat. The belief is that if one eats food without first offering it to God, one will be affected by all the impurities and defects. Sai Baba argues, on the contrary, if you offer the food to the Lord before eating, it becomes (gift from God), and consequently all the impurities in the food are thereby eliminated. This helps the process of gradually cleansing the mind of its impurity or dirt called Mala.

It should, however, be borne in mind that the complete removal of *mala* cannot be done in a day or a month. This requires persistent and prolonged practice. He says that raw gold or ore is to be converted into pure gold; it has to be melted on fire repeatedly to remove the impurities. So also the impurity of man's mind, called "*mala*", can be eliminated only by constant practice over a period of time.

Another distortion of the mind is the constant wavering of the mind, like the movements of the reflected image in a mirror that is kept moving or shaking frequently. To control this waywardness of the mind Sai Baba suggests in the Summer Showers discourse of 1990, one should undertake various spiritual practices like meditation, prayer and the nine modes of devotion mentioned in the scriptures, viz., (1) listening to the Lord's stories, (2) singing His glories, (3) remembrance, (4) service to the Lotus Feet of the Lord, (5) worship, (6) salutation, (7) master-servant relationship, (8) companionship, and (9) offering oneself to the Lord i.e., Self-surrender.

Sai Baba stresses that students should realise that education is for life but not for making a livelihood. They should strain their every nerve to acquire steadiness of mind, which is a prerequisite for concentration. For this, they should bend the body, mend the senses, and end the mind and this is the process of attaining immortality. Sai Baba mentions that if you want to be masters and not slaves, you should keep your body, senses and mind under your control.

Sai Baba asks why the country is today torn by strife, indiscipline, violence, and chaos. It is because people, both young and old, are preoccupied with external material things, totally ignoring the spirit within. The entire educational system is riddled with selfishness. Educated people want to amass wealth quickly by any means, fair or foul, hook or crook. He suggests one's foremost duty is to show gratitude to your parents to whom you owe everything including your food, blood, and head. You have to take care of them, especially in their old age. If you discharge your duties properly and lead your lives on these lines which broaden and purify your minds and hearts, your mind will automatically become free from the distortion of the mind and you will acquire steadiness and concentration of mind without the need for any other spiritual disciplines.

Now, we come to the fourth distortion of the mind which may be likened to a thick cloth covering the mirror of man's mind, which does not at all permit of any reflection whatsoever of the image of the Self. Thus, while *mala* does not enable us to have a clear and correct image of the Self, and while the distortion of the mind results in seeing the Self as wavering, Sai Baba requests that we recognise that what we are experiencing as the real world is only the "reaction", "resound", and "reflection" of your "Real Self." Now, the question arises, "What exactly is the thick cloth that covers the mirror of one's mind"? This cloth is made up of the gang of six internal enemies of man—viz. desire, anger, *greed*, *attachment*, *pride*, and *jealousy* and envy.

Out of the six, pride may be considered as the worst enemy. Pride is of eight kinds: pride of money, learning, caste, affluence, beauty, youth, position or authority, and spiritual pride. If you ponder over two facts you can overcome this enemy namely pride.

Sai Baba advises that if you look around instead of being like a frog in the well, you will find that in respect of each of these eight items that cause pride in you, there are many other people who are superior to you. Secondly, all these items— money, authority, youth etc.—are highly transient. Therefore, get rid of pride as well as the other five enemies included. If you want to remove the cover of your mind's mirror, the best means to remove this thick cloth of *illusion* is to develop love for all. Love is God.

Sai Baba emphasizes that love is the only bond that can unite all and make us realise the one Reality behind all the seeming diversity. A simple illustration will make this point clear. He explains that, you have a candle light. You cover it with a vessel having several holes in it. Although there is one light, you see light through each and every hole, giving the impression of there being several lights. Now, you cover the vessel with a thick cloth. You see no light at all. Next you remove the thick cloth. You see many lights again. Now break or remove the pot. You see the one and only real candle light.

He goes onto say if it is the sense organs that enable a man to see, hear, talk, and so on, how is it that even when all the organs are there intact in a dead person, he is unable to see, hear, talk etc.? It is because the power that animates the organs is not there. The body may be compared to a torch light. The eyes are like the bulbs. The intellect is the switch. If with all these, you don't get light, what could be the reason? Obviously there are no battery cells inside. The blood cells in our body are like those battery cells. They carry the divine energy in them. The blood cells may be there, but if the divine power has left them, they can no longer make the senses function. So it is clear that in the presence of the divine power the body can do many wonders; in its absence, the body becomes not only inert, but also decomposed and rotten.

Sai Baba says another deficiency of the mind is jealousy or envy. It is one of the worst qualities of man. He cannot endure or tolerate the prosperity or happiness of others. There is no cure for this disease. Feel happy when others are happy. Do not give room for envy. Develop fraternal feelings towards your fellow students. Rejoice in their curricular and extra-curricular achievements, without any feeling of envy. The reason for envy is selfishness, which is rampant nowadays both among the students and non-students. For instance, able-bodied students rush in and occupy the front seats in buses, even pushing aside the old people, women, and children who are standing in a long queue. Why don't you give preference to such people? Even if you don't get a seat in the bus, you can afford to walk a mile or two, thereby depriving the double benefit of saving the bus fare and giving much needed exercise to your body.

Sai Baba in this talk to students advises them to follow the following five injunctions

Think no evil; think what is good.

See no evil; see what is good.

Hear no evil; hear what is good.

Talk no evil; talk what is good.

Do no evil; do what is good.

When you adhere to these five injunctions as the very breath of your life, you will be able to overcome all four defects of the mind. We all have private minds, with particular memories and a previous life to contend with as we interact in the world. How can we arrive at solutions with aggression as we have witnessed through all the conflicts and wars that plague society. What happens if our point of departure is love?

PART II

Creating the conditions for Happiness

Almost everybody considers happiness as the greatest pursuit in life. We buy things, have relationships, improve our image and engage in several activities in pursuit of happiness. It is a lifelong quest but based on what we have read so far, happiness remains elusive to the majority of us. We are in a continuous search for that something which will makes us happy. The pharmaceutical industry, psychologists, psychiatrists generate a lot of business attempting to provide some sort of relief to the stresses and strains of life.

The concept of happiness is first introduced to us when we are young. Fairy tales and stories are read to us which creates the impression that happiness exists and most stories conclude with a common theme, they lived happily ever after. This understanding is very uncomplicated and is not a realistic understanding or concept of happiness. Happiness is not an event.

The adverts of products such as cell phones, cars, microwaves and many other commodities creates the impression that purchasing them will result in happiness. No sooner we make the purchase, we seek different and more modern models of these commodities. No amount of money is enough and our lives are constantly characterised by the will to have more. The big question is what makes us happy and can we be happy? One way of creating the conditions for happiness is to develop a more realistic understanding of happiness. This section attempts to provide some clarity on happiness and suggests that we need to be more realistic in our pursuit of happiness. What is very clear is that happiness cannot be bought.

In order for us to create happier lives it is important to understand our minds, what we think, what we desire, what we want, our habits and thoughts as well as all the environmental influences. One of the biggest causes of unhappiness is desire. When we were young, many of us were of the opinion that happiness lasts forever. It does not. I try below to discuss some of the conundrums in our lives and attempt to create a more realistic understanding of happiness.

- Pleasure and Pain
- Desire and Fear
- The mind is a bundle of habits, memories and perceptions
- Our Individual minds is a private world: We have to be flexible
- Understanding the Materialist Age
- Attachment and Detachment
- Leading a contradictory life

Pleasure and Pain

Truth comes into being, when gratifications, the desire for sensation, comes to an end

J Krishnamurthi

One of the most frustrating experiences in life is that pleasure is limited and temporary. Life's experience teaches us that at the background of pleasure lies pain. Training for a marathon is not only about pleasure. There are injuries, bad weather, time constraints and a number of other challenges. The build-up to a marathon involves considerable pain. We will be naïve to assume that distance running is all pleasure. Similarly, all major pursuits that we undertake in life including our careers, marriage and rearing children provide pleasure but also involve pain. Growth, learning and development are often associated with some sort of pain.

In the work and study environment, there are complex personalities and hostile deadlines. Pleasure cannot continue as life always throws challenges to us. We cannot dine and wine for long periods of time or be part of an endless winning streak. The seeking of pleasure is born in pain and often ends in pain. The greatest source of unhappiness is the fact that we seek pleasure and avoid pain. Although the 'pleasure-pain' principle originated in the work of Freud, the father of modern psychoanalysis, one can find traces of its heritage in the work of Aristotle.

> 'We may lay it down that Pleasure is a movement, a movement by which the soul as a whole is consciously brought into its normal state of being; and that Pain is the opposite.

We are born with a *pleasure principle*, that we will seek immediate gratification of needs, for which our bodies reward us with feelings of pleasure. The reverse is also true, and the *pain principle* says that, whilst seeking pleasure people will also seek to avoid pain. The avoidance of pain is the problem as we have to embrace both. On the Lifehack website a commentator had this to say about participants completing the Melbourne Marathon:

When we persevere and do what most people won't (not just in a marathon but with any challenge), we learn, we grow and we change. When we endure the discomfort, face the fear and work through the challenge, we become a better version of us. We get stronger. More courageous, more capable. We develop new skills. We see things differently and we start to produce better results in our world. Why do the vast majority of people who start the marathon complete it? Because they have prepared. They did the work. They got uncomfortable on a consistent basis over an extended period of time. They got fit and strong. They did what the majority wouldn't. They did what needed to be done to produce an exceptional outcome in their world. Marathoner runners understand what it takes to succeed. They understand the concepts of discipline, self-control, and over-coming fear, dealing with discomfort, determination and perseverance. They understand that, more often than not, success has almost nothing to do with potential, age or genetics and everything to do with attitude and hard work. **(My emphasis)**

The above quotation is an illustration of the pleasure pain principle. We need to embrace and accept both pleasure and pain. The quote also captures the characteristics of a strong mind. My experience mentally as a result of running prepares me every-day for the pleasure and pain experiences of life. To expect that every-day is going to pass with pleasure principle is possible if one understands that pain is part of it. It's a part of life's package.

Our pains are relative in a world filled with 7 billion people. Each one charting their own path through this wonderfully and beautifully endowed universe. Pain for one person could be an overdraft and pain for another could be struggling to find where your next meal is coming from. In round numbers there are 7 billion people in the world. Thus, with an estimated 925 million hungry people in the world, 13.1 percent, or almost 1 in 7 people are hungry. One can estimate that 2,128,243,000 individuals in the year 2010 had some sort of cancer. About 700-900 million adults missed education, and about 100 million children don't access school/education. The problems that people in this world are enormous and each one of us should be mindful of these statistics. The level of pain caused by hunger, cancer and a lack of education cannot be measured. We often are too focussed on our own little worlds without considering the broader context.

Accepting both pain and pleasure in life enables one to be happy for great periods of time. There is no greater example of the value of the pleasure pain principle than in running. The ultra-marathons, marathons and half-marathons or even the 10kms have associated with it the pleasure pain principle. The build-up to any race involves great amount of personal sacrifice which often involves many obstacles. Runners persevere and in their life-times run several of these races spending considerable amount of time in preparation and practice. This cycle of practice, running the race, experience of pain and pleasure becomes a cycle of life for almost every runner. Life is no different; we have to accept challenges, distractions and unplanned events. Then only could we be more realistic about what happiness is.

The important lesson we learn from the pain pleasure principle is that we should not quit when the going gets tough. We should get tougher. Quitting at the middle of a marathon means you will not finish the race. Similarly in the work environment, marriage and in rearing our children, we should persevere when things get tough. We take our personalities, our likes and dislikes, perceptions and habits into any environment. Some of these need shaping and reworking if we have to grow and learn. Therefore, for growth and development, adaptation, learning to deal with the bad and good times is indeed a recipe for success.

Desire and Fear

You can live with a few clothes on or with one meal a day but that is not simplicity. Just be simple inwardly

Krishnamurthi J.

Can endless desire for more and more things create the conditions of happiness? How does desire create unhappiness in our lives? We need to draw a distinction between good desires and bad desires. The glut of adverts of iPhones, television sets, new products generate many desires. We spend our lives of earning with the desire of more money. This becomes an endless cycle. Banks also provide loans and companies provide credit facilities. Some people spend their lives paying of debt. Those are bad desires.

From the time we are born we are forced to compete with other children. As life moves on we compete with our colleagues, friends and siblings. As we get older, the competition becomes more intense with our children growing up and as adults the comparisons we make with everybody else consumes our daily lives. We live each day with the thousands of thoughts that shape how we live or how we want to live. The conditions in the world and the factors that stimulate our senses are many. Our challenge is to control our senses and live a quieter, silent life. It is important to be aware of how the senses are impacted upon by different stimuli that result in bad desires.

The 2008 economic crash in the US impacted on all countries in the world. Many people lost their jobs and homes because of greed and speculation by a few. When does greed stop? When does wanting more stop? Understandings and insights into the negative effects of desire will assist us in developing more realistic understandings of happiness.

It is unfortunate that the economic collapse caused by a few greedy bankers resulted in people asking questions about their desires. This event has forced many people to change their lifestyles. The stream of thoughts I mentioned earlier in this book is often about desire. For example, gamblers pursue the next big win without considering the losses incurred. The casinos are always full of people who expect a windfall. When gambling becomes a habit it is often too late. In many cases people work hard to generate more funds with a desire in mind. Often this is accompanied by ill health and other social evils. Forget desire for a moment and witness the silence and the quiet of the mind. Spend a few minutes thinking about the numerous possessions you have. Do we need this? Is it absolutely necessary? Try and become a witness to what is happening around you without getting involved.

Calming the mind has its positive effects and many people have begun this journey, for example, the number of people learning Transcendental Meditation in Canada has increased by over 100% in the last year and a half. Dr Will Overall, director of the Transcendental Meditation organization in Canada, added that interest in the technique is even more pronounced in the larger Canadian cities. For example, he said, more than three times as many people have taken the course in Toronto in the year 2012.

Existing next to desire is fear. We start fearing as soon as we are born. Each of us has our own fears. Fear, like desire consumes almost every second of our lives. There are a multiplicity of fears, which are directed to the unknown. Drawing from many spiritualists in this book we gain safety by virtue of a belief in a higher force.

I sometimes ask myself the question, whether the famous banker in New York is happier than the guy who begs at the traffic light in Cape Town. Where is there more fear and desire? Is it in the banker or the beggar in Cape Town? Whilst I do not want to romanticise the life of the beggar, he/she will greet you with a smile every-time you meet at the traffic light. I often wondered what makes this person smile all the time. What becomes clear to me is that the guy at the traffic light in Cape Town has no burdens, no mortgage and no responsibilities. Very few people will choose that lifestyle but the lesson we can take from the beggar is that we can reduce our desires. Reduced desires results in more peace and silence.

On the other hand you meet your colleagues in management positions who will hardly share a word with you. Busy people hardly ever chat with each other. At airports all over the world, people are on their mobiles, texting or talking. This is a continuous activity. These activities with little time to stand and stare are largely shaped by desire or fear. How many silent moments do we have that is not focussed on acquiring something?

Both desire and fear contribute to a substantial amount of anxiety. Fear of losing one's possessions, fear of losing a personal battle or fear of your children not being successful. I mentioned earlier, a Lou Harris poll found that nearly nine out of ten Americans experience "high" levels of stress. A report from Indiana University says that one quarter of Americans have felt they were on the verge of a nervous breakdown. No wonder that the twenty top-selling drugs in the United States are for depression and anxiety.

There is another type of fear which is creating massive amounts of panic. Countries across the globe are falling apart. With the tension in the Middle East, Afghanistan, and North Africa as well as the economic collapse in Spain and Portugal, many people are leaving their homes or forced to flee. War and economic downturn seems to create the worst kind of fears.

Whilst it is difficult to scale down the effects of wars and economic downturn, it is easier to limit desires and limit fears in a natural environment. It is possible to remove oneself from competition and it is also possible to replace the fear with a confidence. How many thoughts of fear that one has does not materialise? In fact most fears don't materialise and it is important therefore to turn inwards. It is important to attempt to establish where the fear comes from. Fear is often located in the mind. In many cases it is an illusion. Therefore, they say that fear is often a problem of the mind. Take away the mind and the fear disappears. Calming the mind can reduce fears. In a moment of silence and quiet, one is able to work out the origin of these fears.

The section on memory in this book suggests that the fears and desires may come from childhood, experiences during adulthood or it could be influenced from another person's experience that is close to you. In this regard it is important to reflect on the discussion relating to memory and the subconscious in this book. That will provide many answers to why we fear and desire.

In the time just before a big race, many fears surface about injury and almost every reason why things will not go well in the race. Often these mental thoughts manifest themselves as people tend to produce them with negative energy. I had experienced a cold more than once before a race because that was my biggest concern. At one stage I ended up at a sports institute for an examination since I thought I had a runner's knee. Of course, that was not the case. Regarding desire and running, running is a sport that makes you very realistic. If you do a half marathon in 1 hour 44 minutes you are most likely to do a marathon in 4 hours and 10 minutes. You cannot desire to win the race.

Both desire and fear create a substantial amount of activity in the mind that is often counter-productive. It is very important to focus inwards, to observe those thoughts of desire and fear. No desire and no fear can equal calmness. A reduced desire and less fear help one to lead a quieter and more peaceful life.

When passions and desires are silenced, the mind as Einstein advises us can be more creative. When one achieve success for the first time, for example, when you make a big sale, land a good deal, one often develops greed and attempts to increase interest in such things. When one loses, one becomes angry and unhappy. It is desire that ensure people go to casinos, try to land the second big sale or repeat a behaviour that yields some benefit. However, those big gains are seldom repeated in life.

According to Sathya Sai Baba love, goodwill and compassion can be fully satisfied and hence are beneficial to subject and object. Even a small desire can start a long line of action; what about a strong desire? Desire can produce a universe; its powers are miraculous. Just as a small matchstick can set a huge forest on fire, so does a desire light the fires of manifestation. The very purpose of creation is the fulfilment of desire. The desire may be noble or ignoble, space is neutral—one can fill it with what one likes: You must be very careful as to what you desire. And as to the people you want to help, they are in their respective worlds for the sake of their desires; there is no way of helping them except through their desires. You can only teach them to have right desires so that they may rise above them and be free from the urge to create and re-create worlds of desires, abodes of pain and pleasure.

The mind is a bundle of habits, memories and perceptions—Sai Baba

Bearing in mind that our mind-sets are shaped by memories, consciousness and sub-conscious, we are likely to experience frustration when we encounter something different, a different belief, a different view or thinking that is radically different from our frameworks of thinking. High levels of frustration and unhappiness can ensue from our personal mind-sets, habits and perceptions. What we think can result in hostility with others because of our conflicting thoughts. If we have bad habits such as gambling, drugs, narcissism and so on, we tend to reproduce them on a regular basis. In order to make a break or change, we need to be conscious and aware of what is causing our unhappiness. We can go through life repeating our bad habits or we can make a concerted effort to change.

During my reflections I have come to the realisation that if I don't change the way I think in a world where I meet the minds of other people, I will be unhappy. In the world today, most people change jobs a few times. It's a different world that our parents and grandparents lived in. It is a dynamic place that forces us to be flexible and ready for change.

What do we learn from our parents, siblings, peers and people around us? These are the shapers of our future lives. Many of us are dominated by our significant others. When we are young we are taught to compete and we judge ourselves based on other people around us. All of us are socialised in some way by people who we meet. During these processes of meeting others we memorise our experiences through touch, hearing, speaking, feeling and talking. The human being has an extra-ordinary make-up. We can smell a familiar reality decades after we experienced it. Very often we encounter familiar situations much later with a similar response to it. Once we acquire a taste for something, it tends to remain with us for the rest of our lives.

Some argue that we also inherit memories and desires from a previous life. How we are socialised in the formative years, impacts on us as adults. In most cases our parents and peers have a profound impact on our thinking. Within any context it is unlikely for children to view the world differently from the parents. How many people in Nazi Germany defied the status quo? How many people in apartheid South Africa defied the status quo? Of course there are a few but the large majority were aligned with the status quo.

The choice people make regarding material products are largely inherited from their families. Any cohort of people who socialise frequently will generally have similar tastes, likes and dislikes. There are a few who will not align themselves and will rebel but the peer and family pressure forces one to have similar values, ideas and likes. It is a way in which people feel accepted and part of the group. Those who move away and think differently are often ostracized in some way or the other. Therefore generations of families reproduce themselves and if someone steers away from the norm the question will be raised, why you doing it differently or one are will be viewed as odd. If you come from a background where there is considerable amounts unhappiness, you can change by being aware of it.

Memory plays and important role in habit formation that is repeated through generations. If the habits are good and healthy which leads to personal happiness, it is fine. How do we change habits and desires and not repeat the stressful ones that make life difficult for many people in the world? Once again it is about watching and paying careful attention to what we desire and repeat into habits that are harmful to us.

Breaking habits and not repeating them are very difficult if the habit has been entrenched for a period of time. Some habits are influenced by social media and it places enormous pressure on people to conform. The only person who is responsible is the victim. Through the mind major changes can be made. I used running to step away from excess sleeping, particularly on Saturday and Sunday mornings. This decision to get up and enjoy the mountain air or run through the streets of Cape

Town was far more enjoyable than lying in bed. The decision is made in the mind.

Our Individual Minds is a Private World: Be Flexible!

The waters of life are thundering over the rocks of objects—desirable or hateful. Remove the rocks by insight and detachment and the same waters will flow deep and silent and swift, in greater volume and with greater power. Don't be theoretical about it; give time to thought and consideration; if you desire to be free, neglect not the nearest step to freedom.

—I am That

Did you sum up a situation at any stage and find out soon after that your conclusion was wrong? Yes, it happens all the time to most of us. However, we often believe what we think is correct. This is often the root cause of so much of tension between people. It is important to note the impact of memory and sub-conscious on our individual development. We are all wired differently. Aren't we often astonished at the difference amongst siblings in one family?

Through our minds we create little private worlds and prisons as we interact in this universe. What this implies is that each of us, in fact every-one of us lives in a private world. This private world impacts on our lives but also significant others as well as people that we associate with. The damage done to others because of our little prison has far reaching effects not only with the people we work with but their families, children and the careers of people.

The greatest lesson I have learnt is that decisions I take and thoughts I hold are only binding on myself. I often thought that what is in my head is often the truth and realized through this process of reflection, exercise and reading that it is not true. There are no absolute truths when it comes to social phenomena. What we see in the world is a reflection of our memory, sub-conscious, history and life. That is why what many of us assume that what we see into the world constitutes reality. It is our reality. Therefore, it is important to listen to people, be less judgemental and attempt to understand yourself and others in conversations. We all project onto the world what we think. We could be wrong!

In general the older people become, they are more likely to see the world through their own eyes. The world is a set of memories. Depending on which part of the world you come from certain beliefs, regulations and life in general is a memory reproduced. The human race is characterised by difference in terms of race, gender class, ethnicity but also and very importantly, thinking. Often a particular set of beliefs define how people view the world. For example, in 1974 the DSM classification in psychology removed gay people from its classification since it was not regarded as abnormal anymore. This made some people happy and others rejected this change.

Since our minds are a bundle of habits, memories and perceptions, we need to really think about how it shapes our interactions with other people. What we see in the world, be it people, organisations or power dynamics is a reflection of ourselves. If one changes one's work environment, we take ourselves, our memories and our minds to the new environment. We are most likely to experience the same set of frustrations.

The mind based on memory and perceptions builds a particular reality and a view of the world and people. It tends to judge others and events based on our own mental frameworks. This reality that we create can be destroyed. Our minds have certain desires and prompts based on memories and perceptions. On that basis we create habits and desires.

The people who are most successful in this world are those who are ready to change, who are willing to move on and are able to go with the flow of life. An inflexible mind leads to much suffering. Pain is caused by physical events but suffering is caused by a lack of ability to adapt to what requires of you.

When things change around us, we are often threatened and feel uncomfortable. Most of us in times of change are forced to move out of our comfort zones. Each person possesses different characteristics born of different parents, lives in different areas, enjoys a different quality life-style and the differences multiply as one gets older. What is considered to be a truth for one human being could be very different for another.

My running experience has taught me that the only person you compete with is your—self. Each runner has their own history and own potential. Each one trains differently and spends different amounts of times with different goals. I am not going to compete with someone that is training for the

Olympics or become excited when I run past someone in the race whom I don't have knowledge of. Running has helped to move out of my comfort zone of absolute thoughts. Getting up in the morning to train on cold days, running distances beyond what I think I could run and attempting to go beyond myself has forced me to welcome change. I now understand that the world is a social construction and people construct reality. I also am the creator in many instances of my own reality. All these realities are constructed by people, minds and ideas that come from different backgrounds. Therefore, the world is a complex place and to survive it one has to be adaptable. We will be continuously forced to break out of our comfort zones. It is essential that each one of us attempt to break the little prisons that our mind creates. Once again it is a step by step process to watch and observe what the mind thinks.

When we wake up in the morning the mind with its five organs of perception, five organs of action, and five vehicles of consciousness appears as memory, thought, reason and selfhood creates a particular reality says Sr Nisargadatta Maharaj in 'I am That'. The challenge is to realize that the minds projection can be changed at any one time through the mind. In the quotation at the beginning of this book Bhagwan Sri Sathya Sai Baba said that: (i) the mind causes rebirth to beings,

(ii) the mind causes release to beings and (iii) the mind confers victory to beings. We can move out of our comfort zones if we understand that our thoughts create a mental prison. That realization must be a step by step process paying attention to what you think and what is repeated every-day in the mind. The challenge is to break the thought patterns.

Hitler thought that he was right. He attempted to persecute all Jews. It is likely that his actions were the result of his past experiences. His action was shaped by his memory and sub-conscious. Victor Frankl had this to say about his experiences at Auschwitz.

> One man's ideas constructed and propagated violently led to the following conditions that women, children and men had to face in the Holocaust. If only there was an oppositional idea that challenged Hitler's thinking, things would have very different.

Hitler was a leader of a country and his thinking was wrong. The positive aspect of the following conditions was the mind-set change that took place amongst the prisoners.

In the face of death, many "prisoners, changed their mind-sets. Frankl says

> the thought of suicide was entertained by nearly everyone, if only for a brief time. It was born of the hopelessness of the situation, the constant danger of death looming over us daily and hourly, and the closeness of the deaths suffered by many of the others.

Frankl made him-self a firm promise that on the first evening in camp that he would not "run into the wire." This was a phrase used in camp to describe the most popular method of suicide—touching the electrically charged barbed-wire fence. It was not entirely difficult for him to make this decision he says. There was little point in committing suicide, since, for the average inmate, life expectation, calculating objectively and counting all likely chances, was very poor. He could not with any assurance expect to be among the small percentage of men who survived all the selections. The prisoner of Auschwitz, in the first phase of shock, did not fear death. Even the gas chambers lost their horrors for him after the first few days—after all, they spared him the act of committing suicide.

Therefore, people can use their minds to free themselves. They can liberate themselves in the face of oppression or trying circumstances. Many people in the world complain about change. Why are people so frustrated by change? Why is it difficult for human beings to adapt? Often we do not admit that your conclusions bind nobody but ourselves. It is possible that the image we see could be totally wrong. Our problem is that the image we have our-selves and our situations could be wrong as well.

According to the One Minute Meditator, despite our huge potential for fresh thinking, our mind mostly repeats over and over. In spite of flashes of creativity, we largely step from one time-worn piece of mental turf to the next. We deepen decades-old ruts minute after minute after minute. At any given time, the best and worst of our thinking bubbles nonstop in our heads.

The world has witnessed many atrocities because of some single minded powerful people who were wrong. Saddam Hussein, George Bush, Tony Blair and Hitler are some of them. Hitler's destruction of the Jewish people must go down in history as one of the most inhumane acts of aggression against ordinary people. His mind and thoughts were put into action resulting in the death of so many innocent women, children and men. Saddam Hussein's destruction of the Kurdish people and George Bush and Tony Blair's involvement in Iraq can also be regarded as inhuman. We also have smaller versions of these people who think that what is in their heads is the truth. The diversity of the world should teach all of us respect and tolerance.

Man is a social being and as such we have to interact with the private world of every person. It follows that each one of us should be tolerant, forgiving, less judgemental and supportive. Sai Baba says that the mind is also referred to as self. In truth, it is an illusion. Everyone says, I am mentally worried, my mind is troubling much but has one seen this mind. No one knows what the mind is, but they suffer from the mind, from its illusory existence. The worry which you suffer is your own creation. Fear too is self-creation. When we imagine the mind is there, it shows up. Deny it or enquire into it, it vanishes totally. Instead of enquiring, we give the mind undue prominence and allow it to ride over us and subject ourselves to suffering. However, this is a long and time consuming process. It requires total dedication and application to every thought that one encounters. Once again every thought in the mind should be monitored and one should be conscious of all the time. Like a marathon each step counts and focus has to be precise.

For individuals to make progress they have to regulate the mind. Habit, desire and repetition may characterise most human beings. If one has habits and desires that lead to minimal frustration, it is fine. If one recognizes mere habit, built on memory, prompted by desire, you will think yourself to be a person. Sai Baba is very clear here when he says that our good and bad luck are linked to our thoughts. The mind immerses man in impenetrable darkness through bad thoughts. The same mind can lift man to sublime heights by good thoughts. Thus thoughts are supremely important for man. They constitute his life breadth. Without understanding this truth, man allows evil tendencies like anger, envy, hatred and conceit to fill his mind and thereby courts disaster. The mind wills, yearns, prompts and insists on effort and action. These are likely commands. Everyone one has to be aware of the variety and validity of the actions induced by these promptings. The mind is host to 50 million such. Of the thoughts that appear and vanish, the clouds pass silently many stay and stir the mind into activity.

Understanding The Materialist Age

Juliet B. Schor in writing about the Overspent American says that millions of us face difficult choices every-day. Many of us spend beyond what we can afford. For example, people in one-earner families find themselves trying to live the lifestyle of their two-paycheck friends. Some parents of who do not have the means struggle to pay for the private schooling that others in their reference group have established as the right thing to do for their children.

Schor argues that more challenges for consumers are created by the accelerating pace of product innovation. Marketing strategies have been changed by manufacturers who prey on both rich and poor. Gourmet cereal, a luxurious latte, or bathroom fixtures that make a statement, the right statement, are offered to people almost everywhere on the economic spectrum. Through the use of credit cards, anyone can buy designer anything, at the trendiest retail shop or at outlet prices. That's the new consumerism. Schor says this is very difficult to resist. We must be aware that this consumerism can be the greatest source of our unhappiness.

Corporatism has taken hold all over the world. It is influencing almost every aspect of our lives. Most political parties and politicians are corporatized. There are very few journalists that tell the truth as they are influenced by particular dogmas that need to be told if they have to be successful. Virtually all human interactions have been shaped by the culture of materialisation. Those people who want to tell the truth are marginalized.

Schor goes onto point out our contradictory lifestyle when she says that part of what's new is that lifestyle aspirations are now formed by different points of reference. For many of us, the neighbourhood has been replaced by a community of co-workers, people we work alongside and colleagues in our own and related professions. And while our real-life friends still matter, they have been joined by our media "friends." (This is true both figuratively and literally—the television show Friends is a good example of an influential media referent.) We watch the way television families live, we read about the lifestyles of celebrities and other public figures we admire, and we consciously and unconsciously assimilate this information. It affects us.

A few centuries ago, money was not in existence. As soon as people learnt that they could produce goods and services and sell them for money, a very different life faced human beings. Material accumulation has shaped our lifestyles to a very significant degree. Almost each second through our cell phones, other forms of media, we are pounded with a range of stimuli. This stimuli sets us up for desire, competition, envy, greed and malice. People are often judged on material accumulation and levels of success between individuals, communities and countries vary. However, the most powerful are those who are viewed as rich. Each person attempts to compete with the next person. Unfortunately everybody's desires cannot be met and this leads to frustration, anger, theft and sometimes suicide.

I mentioned earlier that desires are the greatest source of our unhappiness. Whilst we are unable to go into the forests and meditate, we have to take care of our responsibilities in the real world. I have no doubt that happiness can be achieved if we draw from spiritual teachings both from the west and east. The theme that pervades most spiritual teaching is love and the need to curtail desires.

Young and old people fall prey to consumer industry. Margaret Thatcher monetized the world but the capitalist age has laid the foundation for judging how good and competent people are based on wealth. Another dimension to this competitive edge is the will to perform and demonstrate how good one is in terms of money, power and sex. In this process the values of yesteryear and the values brought about by spirituality plays second fiddle to ego, dominance greed and power.

Sai Baba warns us that the mind wills, yearns, prompts and insists on effort and action. These are likely commands and often we are prompted by desires of ego, dominance, power and sex. Everyone one has to be aware of the variety and validity of the actions induced by these promptings. The mind is host to 50 million such. We must be constantly aware of what we think and desire. Are they good or bad desires?

A large number of politicians are controlled by big capital to a large extent and the small minority of the very rich dictates the world's affairs. The human element is secondary to an oppressive ideology that is self-centred. This world exists for the majority of one's working life. The social construction of the world by people in power who are often referred to as the 1% in the US dictate the agenda for 7 billion people. Some politicians and other leaders in society are pawns of the neo-liberal world. The workers on the ground and their children appear to be insignificant in the majority of countries. One can ask the questions, why do so many people suffer in a world with so many resources? Why do the children of people who build our roads perform the worst in Maths and Language when they build the safe roads that we drive on? This is the way of the 21st century, a place of doom for the poor and dispossessed. This is a dominant theme in most countries. It does not have to be this way.

The manner in which the world is structured in the materialist age creates a suitable climate for unhappiness and disillusionment in the lives and particularly in the minds of people. As this section of the book will illustrate it is not only individuals that are at fault but the materialist age. The age of materialism can trap us into servitude or we could rise about it. It depends entirely on how you think and what you do about it. The most obvious result of living in this age is that one could become a victim. Alternatively, if you understand your context, discourage bad desires and empower your mind, you will have higher levels of happiness.

We often link wealth to happiness. According to Aneki. com (2013), the happiest countries are Nigeria, Mexico, and Venezuela. This website also indicates that the countries with the highest alcohol rates are Luxembourg, France, Ireland and Portugal. Japan and Slovenia have the highest suicide rates. Analyses of these countries tell us that whilst Japan is an economic power it has the highest suicide rate and Nigeria, Mexico and Venezuela are middle to lower income countries but are the happiest. It is interesting that Luxembourg, France and Ireland enjoy the status of highest alcohol rates. What this all means is that economic power is not linked to happiness. Of course you need a level of stability and security but wealth is not consistent with happiness. In the case of Japan it seems that this highly industrialized nation with a great aspiration and desire for wealth is not a happy country.

In fact the consumer culture is becoming an international problem. Michael Richardson in the New York Times wrote in 1994 that Across Southeast Asia, government officials, educators and religious leaders are starting to count the cost of the region's rapid economic growth, wrenching social change and rampant materialism. They are becoming increasingly worried at signs of eroding moral values. Richardson indicates that in a survey of 5,860 youths, aged 13 to 21, showed that 71 percent smoked, 40 percent watched pornographic videos, 28 percent gambled, 25 percent drank alcohol and 14 percent took hard drugs. He argues that the spread of consumer culture—fanned by television and advertising, much of it influenced by Western trends and ubiquitous international media technology—is blamed for a decline of parental control and core family ethics.

Jim Ryun, former record holder of the mile in the US, said the new materialism was costing the nation its stature in international track because the goals of some American athletes are to "make a lot of money or have a nice car."

In the Catholic World News in March 2012, Archbishop Nienstedt argues that believers must strive against materialism. He says "American culture is characterized by a heightened individualism, a rampant secularism and a pervasive hedonism that tends to consider the self-first, acquaintances second and the stranger last," he said during a wide-ranging interview whose topics included the financial crisis, religious freedom, and social media. "The Church must be reawakened in the United States and Catholics need to learn—for only then will they love—their faith. And then, like the Christians of every age, our proclamation of saving truths will become performative: the world will know that we are Christians by our love."

We have lost track of our internal selves and are focussing outwards seeking happiness where it may not exist. When does all this stop. Sai Baba's quote is very useful here, the mind is said to be instrument of liberation and bondage, if the mind extroverts its senses, it becomes the reason for bondage. By the inspiration of the intellect if the mind introverts to seek happiness then it becomes an instrument to liberate itself.

Whenever I bought a new cell phone it was quite refreshing to see all the new gadgets and applications. The same thing applied to my children. After a while it loses its novelty. The same applies to my car and clothes. The novelty wears out very quickly. What is sustained happiness, happiness that gives you the reassurance that you are well? That is the important aspiration I think.

To move from the external to the internal requires a mind shift but one has to be constantly aware of the mind's prompts towards desires of an external nature. When one focuses inward and listen to the silence of the mind, answers regarding peace flow. We must be constantly vigilant about the information and advertising we are exposed to. Does it contribute to our peace and happiness or is it taking us down the road to destruction?

Attachment and Detachment

If one allows a problem to endure, it distorts the mind

—Krishnamurthi J

I have learnt that detachment is one of the most difficult pursuits yet most rewarding. Often what we are most attached to creates the most pain. There are many people in our social lives and at work that make our lives very difficult. You probably experienced this as well. For some reason we form an attachment to certain people who present us with tough emotional and related challenges. We socialise with them but they appear to bring out the worst in us at an emotional level. At this stage I am unsure why I get very close to certain people that make me feel miserable. Very often this is about our unfulfilled needs that attract us to certain people. In the light of the discussion on memory and the sub-conscious it does make sense that there are definite reasons for our collaboration or socialisation. Whenever, I experienced this phenomena I tried detachment and it worked. However, it is not a simple task of detaching oneself from another person. It requires steady mind training. After a period of time, one witnesses the results.

There are other forms of attachment and much of this is at a material level. In life we have the choice of attaching ourselves to transitory and impermanent experiences, items and episodes. The glut of products that are advertised and all the other material possessions I referred to earlier, provides momentary pleasure and after a while lose its novelty. As mentioned earlier, happiness is not a temporary episode or event. It is a process and it involves mind training. We always have to ask the big question, does this matter to me in the long-term?

There are other temporary episodes in life, for example, an argument, a disagreement or a personal attack on your self-worth. These temporary episodes and transient experiences may or may not influence one's self worth at a particular point in time. It depends entirely on one's attitude. One has to ask the question, is this relevant or of any concern over the long-term? However, practicing detachment at a personal or emotional level requires self-knowledge, awareness and being conscious of what one thinks.

Practising detachment from the things we are attached to is the first step of letting go and moving on. Juliet B. Schor introduces a useful concept titled downshifters and argues that not everyone is going along with the new consumerism. The pressures for upscale consumption, and the work schedules that go along with it, created millions of exhausted, stressed-out people who started wondering if the cycle of work and spend was really worth it. And some concluded that it wasn't. So they started downshifting, reducing their hours of work and, in the process, earning and spending less money.

She argues that downshifters are opting out of excessive consumerism, choosing to have more leisure and balance in their schedules, a slower pace of life, more time with their kids, more meaningful work, and daily lives that line up squarely with their deepest values. Schor says that downshifters can be found at all income levels, from the comfortable suburbanites whose homes are paid for, to those who are counting every penny, resigned to the fact that they'll never own a home. Their jobs were leaving them drained, depressed, or wondering what life is all about. Now they may not have as much money, but they are spending every day answering that all-important question. And they are much happier. She mentions that some downshifters were compulsive shoppers, mired in credit card debt with little of value to show for it, or caught up in competitive consumption that had spiralled way above what their means could support. Some are kids, just out of college, farsighted enough to avoid the blind alleys taken by older siblings or parents.

Detachment from careers, material possessions, people who are negative is crucial for happiness. I learnt while running that we spend so much of time thinking about things that we are attached to. If it is taken away, for example in a natural disaster, there is nothing you can do. When you die you leave the earth with nothing, all the possessions and people that are attached to disappear. Whilst living we should attempt to create the conditions of authentic joy.

Leading a Contradictory Life

Most people will argue that one of their main pursuits in life is to obtain peace of mind or creating the conditions for happiness. Whilst this is the main pursuit, the action of individuals and their daily practice contradict their peaceful intention. The fact that many of us are: (i) pleasure seeking; (ii) have desires; (iii) lacking self-knowledge; (iv) victims of the materialist age and; (v) having great sense of attachment to people, happiness remains elusive. In a sense, the pursuit of happiness is compromised by a life that is prone to unhappiness. The biggest challenge that face most people relate to how they interact with other people. In the workplace, sports events and in socialisation, we must come to terms with the fact that what we think may not be correct. There is a tendency for people to dominate others with their thoughts and ideas. As a result we find ourselves in very hostile social situations. It is very important that we realize our thinking is a mere contribution to debates and discussions. It is not the absolute truth.

We want peace but our actions in pursuit of peace are contradictory. To obtain the level of peace and to pursue happiness, we have to be conscious of our thought patterns and what we practice. When there is harmony between thinking, action and practice, one is moving in the direction of the peace we want. If there is tension or a contradiction between thinking and practice, we have to ask question, do we really want to experience calmness and peace?

I have mentioned throughout this publication that this is not an easy task. It requires a conscious decision and action if success is to be achieved. The discussion in this part of book helps one to understand the challenges associated with creating the conditions of happiness. Happiness is a relative term and could mean different things to different people. The challenge is to create a realistic understanding of happiness within the confines of one's personal life. We have to remember that we are products of a particular history that has shaped who and what we are. We have strengths and limitations and the challenge is to make the necessary changes to create the conditions for happiness.

PART III

Training the Mind

To have inward solitude and space implies freedom to be, to go, to fly

J Krishnamurthi

It was mentioned earlier on in this book that one way of subduing the mind is to be conscious of your thoughts every second, minute and day or repeat a mantra as well as invoke the name of God's. Reference is also made to the value of practice, what ever you practice is what you become good at.

Subduing the mind cannot happen without significant effort. In fact the more conscious you are of your thoughts and by increasing your experience of silence, the stronger your mind grows. I also mentioned that I started this about 8 years ago and I am pursuing this method with more rigour because I am experiencing success. From my experiences running more than 13 000 kilometres, I am yet to achieve the progress that I would have liked. The feelings of joy and happiness are more frequent than they have ever been. I am able to not become emotionally attached to many of my thoughts and I have developed the ability to detach myself from them. Remarkably, when people irritated me it did consume a lot of my time in the past. More recently, this is something I deal with calmly at most times. The advantage is that I frequently refer to this body of knowledge when under pressure.

In any conversation, I have realized that my thoughts and input are merely contributions. There is hardly ever a right or wrong. However, there is much more to do. The toing and froing from good moods to not so good moods continues but the will is one of determination to subdue and overcome the negative stuff. The big and quick gains have been my positive attitude to most occurrences. For example, I decided in all the half marathons that I will reach a specific time. I did it on each occasion. At the start of the New York Marathon and the London Marathon I said that I will finish both races. I did it despite injuries before and during the race. The relationship between the mind and achievement is clear to me. The relationship between the mind and behaviour is also evident to me. The mind shapes everything.

Very useful advice can be extrapolated from the work of Malcolm Gladwell and Eckhart Tolle. In Malcolm's book Outliers he makes reference to the 10 000 hour rule and in Eckhart's book, the Power of Now, he invokes the powerful concept of focussing on the now or the present. Both the 10 000 hour rule and focussing on the now are vital ingredients for success if one wants to create a calmer mind.

Whilst Malcolm speaks about the ingredients for successful people, the application of the ten thousand hour rule can be applied to train the mind. Happiness is not an event. A calm mind is not an event. Both are long processes that require intense commitment and dedication over a considerable period of time. In the case of focussing on the present, one of the major distractions is thinking about the future or the past. Most people you speak to will either speak about the future or the past. Reflect on what you are thinking right now. How many of us focus on the present. Focussing on the present is a very powerful tool to assist in mind training.

Gladwell asks the question, is the ten thousand hour rule a general rule for success? He answers this by arguing that if we scratch below the surface of every great achiever, it seems that the ten thousand hour rule works. Citing the Beatles, John

Lennon, Paul Mc Cartney, George Harrison and Ringo Starr, Malcolm explains their discipline through the comments of John Lennon.

> We got better and got more confidence, we couldn't help it with all the experience playing all night long. We had to try even harder, put our heart and soul into it, to get ourselves over. . . . In Hamburg, we had to play for eight hours, so we really had to find a new way of playing.

The Beatle's drummer Pete Best confirms the discipline when he says

> we played seven nights a week. At first we played non-stop till twelve-thirty when it closed, but as we got better the crowds stayed till two most mornings seven days a week.

Bill Gates provides a similar story about discipline and commitment. Computers were his obsession, he says. I skipped athletics and I went up there at night referring to the computer centre at the University of Washington. It would be a rare week that we do not get 20 to 30 hours a week.

In the Power of Now, Eckhart Tolle, reminds us about the value of focussing on the moment. He asserts:

Are you worried? Do you have any "what ifs" thoughts? Eckhart says you are identified with your mind, which is projecting itself into an imaginary future situation and creating fear. He says there is no way that you can cope with such a situation, because it doesn't exist. It's a mental phantom he argues. You can stop this health and life-corroding insanity simply by acknowledging the present moment he advises. Become aware of your breathing, feel the air flowing in and out of your body. Feel your inner energy field. All that you ever have to deal with, cope with, in real life—as opposed to imaginary mind projections—is this moment. Ask yourself what "problem" you have right now, not next year, tomorrow, or five minutes from now. What is wrong with the moment Eckhart asks? You can always cope with the Now, but you can never cope with the future—nor do you have to.

He adds further that the strength, the right action or the resource will be there when you need it, not before, not after. We have learnt about the complexity of the mind which is exacerbated by living in the 21st century with all its impositions. A constant vigilance of the prompts of the minds and the thoughts that emerge is a first step. The second and subsequent steps will involve calming the mind and changing negative thoughts to positive thoughts. A dedicated campaign to become detached from the emotions of thoughts is essential so that the mind does not get carried away in mindlessness.

Too many of us are concerned about little things that pass that are quite irrelevant in the bigger picture of life. It is very important to understand what is temporary or transient. One will have to ask oneself the question, how this affects me in ten years-time? Fortunately, most experiences in life are of a transient nature. We meet a rude person, or we hear some bad gossip about ourselves or we lose a cell phone. All these things are transient and temporary. Let go of them quickly. Do not allow your mind to hold onto negative experiences of a transient nature. It is a total waste of energy and time.

In this section, some issues are discussed with regard to training the mind. These include, controlling the senses, changing one's attitude, being quiet and projecting powerful thoughts as well meditation

Control the senses: This is important!

You must watch yourself continuously— particularly your mind—moment by moment, missing nothing.

—I am that

Watching your mind each step of the way is key to trying to understand it and mastering it. If you miss one step you will not reach the summit or finish the Marathon of the Mind.

The advice from I am That is that we must watch ourselves continuously—particularly our minds—moment by moment, missing nothing in order to calm the mind. Whilst one of our main goals is to calm the mind, we must note that in order to control the senses we have to understand that it is continuously exposed to a range of stimuli. We have to deal with all the incoming stimuli on a daily basis. To sift out what is transient and temporary, what is totally irrelevant and what is important requires discrimination and use of the intellect. As humans we possess an intellect which is crucial to the survival of the human race.

What is most apparent in this digital age is that there is so much of information that could be quite overwhelming. Given the information from the One Minute Meditator about the number of thoughts we have and the section on memory about how we process and retain information, it is very evident that human beings are presented with challenges never experienced before.

Sai Baba offers great wisdom regarding the pranks of the mind.

> It is not easy to subdue the mind immediately. But you must begin to bring it under control. When the mind desires something, you must immediately set the intellect at work. Why? So that the intellect may give you proper advice. The mind has to be taught the lesson: Oh Mind Don't plays your petty pranks. Examine your desire to find out if it is good or bad, right or wrong. **Do not wish to acquire whatever you desire. (my emphasis)**

In the past we heard information from people and newspapers. Now, we have the internet, email and other forms of social media. Whilst people were challenged in the past with limited information, the 21st century knowledge explosion is something that we should take seriously if we want to ensure good and sound mental health. The crucial question here is what is the possible impact of this information age on our development? What happens to people who are born today (as part of the digital age) and live for the next sixty years? What are their likely mind-sets in forty years? These are questions we will not be able to answer since the impact of the information has not been measured in these terms.

My view is that in the information age, we should be disciplined and not distracted. Distraction will increase as our exposure to information increases. This is becoming evident if one measures reading and writing progress amongst young children at an international level. Children do not read and write as much as they used to. What kind of future society are we looking at? Our alternative is to control the senses and this is probably the most important intervention that we will make. If our minds work the way Sandersen says in terms of processing and if we have thousands of thoughts a day, what will be the impact of cell phones and emails on our ability to function over an extended period of time?

From 2008, international media has exposed the level of debt that has been incurred by large numbers of people. The constant exposure to stimuli in the form of adverts can be a huge problem to large numbers of people. The mental health of many of us will suffer as a result of level of exposure to things that are available but we may not be able to afford. It is not surprise that when many of the youth that rioted in the UK recently went for designer labels and designer stores when they looted. They see these things regularly on television and on their cell-phones but they cannot afford it.

Now more than ever before we need to calm the mind and find time to exercise. It is also important to be aware of how the senses can be manipulated by a glut of information. We have to learn to have the ability to discriminate and detach ourselves from a substantial body of information that is at our disposal. According to Sai Baba the mind is a cauldron of prompts and desires. It is a conglomeration of thoughts of various kinds. Sometimes when the thoughts become exciting, it gets upset and throws itself into grief. But in truth, it is just a bundle of thoughts. Just as the many threads spun together make up the cloth, so also the many thoughts make the mind. No thought, no mind either.

We need to make this the age of exercise and meditation to counter the negative effects of the information age on our sense. Mind control and mind training is an essential ingredient for equipoise and tranquillity. Now, more than ever before we need to make a definite attempt to control the senses.

Regarding the senses Sai Baba has some very good advice,

> The mind activates the eye and ear, the tongue and nose and every organ of perception and action. The mind initiates its activation when a prompt influences it. The decisions which the mind makes, either to commit or omit are amazing, for, the Cosmos and all its contents can be described as their consequence. The mind decides on the fact or facet of the objective world which it has to notice. The prompt bears fruit and the fruit conforms to the seed from which it springs. It has to reveal its impact sooner or later. So, man has to avoid evil prompts and cultivate good ones.

Sai Baba says therefore, as soon as a passing thought sprouts in the mind as an urge or desire, one has to examine it with care to discover whether it would tarnish or promote one's reputation, hinder or help one's progress, weaken or strengthen one's character. If it is of the former category cast it away, as a foul stinking object. And, save yourself by saturating the mind with good intentions. Unrest, anxiety and anarchy are bed by evil prompts. You must see good, hear good and act good, so that evil intentions do not arise. The mind travels quicker than sound, far quicker than even light.

In order to survive and create the conditions for happiness, introspection is required concerning desires and habits. Whilst the temptations are great, the rewards of a disciplined life are key to happiness. Because of language and the ability to learn from history, human beings quickly realize the value of moderation and refinement of the senses as we grow older.

As humans I believe we have a purpose amongst 7 billion fellow beings. We are born in diversity and confronted with various cultures, countries and languages. We spend a short period of time and relative to the duration of the universe of about 4 billion years, our stay is very short. What is our purpose here? Surely it has to do with becoming more refined human beings. How this is possible and what do we have to do? We are separated from other species through culture and language. Cursory analyses of cultures suggest in each culture a deep and wonderful commitment to the divine. Each culture speaks of tolerance, love, moderation and helping one another. The world's population is in distress with fifty percent living in poverty. Alcohol and drug abused coupled with human trafficking as well as other social evils suggests we have a long way to go in terms of following the moderate and peaceful life suggested by all scriptures be in Buddhist, Christian or Hindu?

Change your attitude

Based on what has been written in this book up till now, one can clearly see the relationship between attitude and the mind? Having said that, I find it quite remarkable how people differ in their attitude. My view is that attitude is shaped by exposure and knowledge. To know what is possible requires some insight and knowledge. As I prepared for both the New York and London Marathons, I met people with a lot of insight into running. My running mate Vincent Ciolli provided me with so much of information on the use of energy in running. We used to run up the mountain at Constantia Nek in Cape Town on Sundays. It is a 16km run up the mountain which was very demanding. While we ran Vince used to talk to me about using gravity when running and he spoke extensively on a range of topics which made me realize that the information on running is extensive. There is a solution for almost every injury and challenge when it comes to running. We also did a four and a half hour trek from Simonstown to Hout Bay over the mountains and each step of the way, Vince spoke with great authority on the mechanics of running. Vince had a library of information in his head. The more information I received, the more confident I became. So my sense is that there is a clear relationship between attitude and knowledge. The positive attitude comes out of knowing that there is something out there that you want to reach and you can reach it.

Arguably, there is also a mysterious element to attitude. Who are the most positive people? What kind of attitude does it take to fall and wake up again in to face another challenge? Who are the people that do not sweat the small stuff? What kind of attitude does it take to take a penalty at a soccer match in front of 60 to 100 000 people? It seems attitude is also impacted upon by confidence. One has to be confident about something to have a positive attitude. Both knowledge and confidence are interrelated. My sense is that they are inextricably linked. However. the mind must play a crucial role in shaping attitude. I strongly believe that the level of control that one has over one's mind is the ultimate shaper of attitude. What makes someone walk across the grand-canyon on a tightrope and how can someone at the age of 64 swim from Cuba to Florida? In both these cases, these individuals have a very firm grip on their minds. They have to a large extent calmed their minds and focused it.

For those of us who are novices and are learning the ropes of calming the mind, we have to practice the 10 000 hour rule and focus on the present. A point of departure should be focus on the mind. We will not get out of the starting blocks if there is no focus. Calming the mind, deciding on a goal, increasing the knowledge will shape confidence and the attitude. The confidence increases with time and practice.

Attachment, desire and fear, memory, thinking, perceptions shape repetitive behavior and habits. We must be alert to what we think and find those repetitive thought patterns that create negativity. Initially, it will be very difficult but a stand has to be taken at some point to change one's attitude towards negative thought processes. Having an understanding of the mind and memory is crucial as well as one's own idiosyncrasies. One has to break the pattern of negative thinking. However, the awareness of the mind is a useful point of departure. Once again this is a step by step process and not an event,

Person made pleasures, desire and all forms of influences produce a person. If we are objects we will be victims forever.

We are not objects; we have the ability to change our life. Human agency is a major characteristic of human beings which is the ability to do something about your situation. Addiction to pleasure, at whatever cost, is so universal that there must be something significant at the root of it as I had discussed earlier. All this can be changed by recognizing the patterns and trying to make a change. That is the first step. Increasing knowledge about what you want to change is as important. That will give you the confidence to move forward.

Be quiet

I mentioned earlier the knowledge explosion of the 21st century. An incident in Beijing or New York can be seen the next minute in Cape Town. Some people are recipients of more than two hundred e-mails and text messages a day. What does this mean for the mental health of people? I mentioned earlier that the impact of this one's mental health over one's lifespan will not be known for a while. More information will become available about the full impact when this current younger generation reach a senior age. However, what we are picking up is that many young people are reading and writing less.

What is the impact on such activities on the mind which is already churning out thousands of thoughts each minute? It is quite obvious that there will be more pressure and the likely outcome is that people are less like to possess focus and concentration. Reading and writing less on the part of children could be attributed to a lack of focus and concentration.

According to the dialogues of Sr Nisargadatta Maharaj if you could only keep quiet, clear of memories and expectations, you would be able to discern the beautiful pattern of events. It is your restlessness that causes chaos he argues. This is indeed very powerful advice as we get entrenched into the information age. Restlessness and chaos is bound to increase as technology advances. This is similar to the discourse of the Power of Now. Be in the moment! Eckhart Tolle confirms this when he says, presence is needed to become aware of beauty, the majesty, the sacredness of nature. Eckhart asks

> have you ever gazed up into the infinity of space on a clear night, awestruck by the absolute stillness and inconceivable vastness of it? Have you listened, truly listened, to the sound of a mountain stream in the forest? Or to the song of a blackbird at dusk on a quiet summer eventing? To become aware of such things, the mind

needs to be still. You have to put down for a moment your personal baggage of problems, of past and future, as well as all your knowledge, otherwise you will see but not see, hear but not hear. Your total presence is required.

There can be no better advice than that which comes from the Power of Now on this subject. I have struggled with this concept for a long time but I think Sr Maharaj and Eckhart Tolle are right when they say if you just try to keep quiet, all will come—the work, the strength for work, the right motive. Must you know everything beforehand? Don't be anxious about your future—be quiet now and all will fall in place. The unexpected is bound to happen, while the anticipated may never come. Don't tell me you cannot control your nature. You need not control it he says. Throw it overboard. Have no nature to fight, or to submit to. No experience will hurt you, provided you don't make it into a habit. Of the entire universe you are the subtle cause. All is because you are. Grasp this point firmly and deeply and dwell on it repeatedly. To realise this as absolutely true, is liberation. This is a very powerful message by Sr Maharaj and I have realized that one has to be absolutely committed to this notion. Think about your own life and your own experiences. Think about your work if you work and think about the people you meet and have met. Try and work out how your life has progressed. Don't be anxious about your future. Just do well!

Sr Maharaj when being interviewed by a devotee in I am That says you want immediate results! We do not dispense magic here. Everybody does the same mistake: refusing the means, but wanting the ends. You want peace and harmony in the world, but refuse to have them in yourself. Follow my advice implicitly and you will not be disappointed. I cannot solve your problem by mere words. You have to act on what I told you and persevere. It is not the right advice that liberates, but the action based on it. Just like a doctor, after giving the patient an injection, tells him: 'Now, keep quiet. Do nothing more, just keep quiet,' I am telling you: you have got your 'injection', now keep quiet, just keep quiet. You have nothing else to do. My Guru did the same. He would tell me something and then said: 'Now keep quiet. Don't go on ruminating all the time. Stop. Be silent'.

This I think is the most powerful message anyone can get but it is one of the biggest challenges we face particularly in these times.

Projecting Powerful Thoughts

What we visualise can happen! We heard that our minds are a bundle of habits and desires. We tend to reproduce the status quo over and over again since we are wired in particular ways. Human beings also differ from most other creatures since they have an intellect and can discriminate. We do possess human agency which can result in change. What we visualise can happen! What we also know is that nothing happens without an effort. It is critical that we pay very careful attention to what we think. That is the crux of the matter. What we think is what we are.

Road Running and spirituality has taught me powerful lessons about projecting powerful thoughts. Distances I ran and the speeds I accomplished were only possible through thinking it is possible.

Try to visualize daily. Often what you think can happen if you apply your mind. During the run up to all of my races, I ran the race in my mind if I knew the route. I did the Two Oceans half marathon in 2010 running under five minutes for every kilometre. I ran that race in my mind a hundred times. On the day, nothing mattered since I visualised the race and the finish. The same principle was applied to the New York Marathon. The law of expectation is strange but true. Believe in it!

Sr Nisargadatta Maharaj found that thoughts become self-fulfilling; things would fall in place smoothly and rightly. Think about where you are right now and how you got there. What was your desire and was your desire fulfilled. Think also about where you want to be! It does not have to be restricted to any specific issues. Each one of us has different goals and we may want to work on some area of our life. Whatever you want to do, you have to begin with the mind and project in your mind what you want done. Then work towards it!

Meditation

Our minds are scripted in a sense. Each of us is in our own paradigms. It is like listening to different songs, that is how each of us is. We struggle to break free as life, our histories, memories, habits perceptions put us into a particular box. It is like a rat that is spinning on a wheel in a cage. That is our everyday routine. We get up in the morning and think certain thoughts. How do those thoughts differ tomorrow and the next day. It is virtually the same pattern with different scenarios.

These thought patterns prevent us from saying yes to Ekhart Tolle when he asks the following questions:

> Have you listened, truly listened, to the sound of a mountain stream in the forest? Or to the song of a blackbird at dusk on a quiet summer eventing? To become aware of such things, the mind needs to be still.

Given this scenario, it does not matter whether we live in Cape Town, Sahara desert or San Francisco. We will not be able to appreciate the beauty of Table Mountain in Cape Town or the beauty of the sea. Our minds take care of that because it is consumed by thoughts and more thoughts every minute. For us to listen to the mountain stream or hear the birds chirping outside in morning we have to be attentive to what our first thoughts are in the morning. What are we thinking? What do we think tomorrow? Watch the pattern. This cycle has to be ruptured. Practice thinking something different and look at the resistance of the mind. It will become a contest between the dominant thinking and the new thinking. What can be quite useful as a starting point is to meditate. According to the

One Minute Medidator, many people have found meditation useful for controlling the mind. They suggest Five Breaths. Start by settling comfortably in your seat. Close your eyes. Slowly, deeply draw in a breath. Feel your chest rise and your belly expand. Inhale until you feel your lung tissue stretch and flood with oxygen. Now exhale slowly. Let your chest relax, your belly go limp. Then take four more breaths the same way.

Your breathing can rupture your thinking patterns and create the conditions for calming the mind. Why? According to the One Minute Meditator, because, believe it or not, your mind follows your breath. As you deliberately savor the cool air flowing in, and feel the warm air coursing out, you slow the flow of your thoughts and emotions. As you slow your breath, you soothe your mind.

Part IV

The Ingredients for
Creating a Calmness of the Mind

Remember the 10 000 hour rule I mentioned earlier. As the old adage goes, practice makes perfect. After several thousand kilometres and daily if not (secondly) awareness of my thought patterns, I do have a tendency to lose focus from time to time. Physical, Mental and Spiritual exercises are inextricably linked together. Patience and persistence, being conscious of one's thoughts and applying the 10 000 rule to everything you do is crucial to one's success in calming the mind. It is a long process which requires constant dedication. Whenever you fall, get up and try again. You are bound to have challenges and the constant chatter in your mind may suggest that it is not working. Trust me, after some time, you will notice the progress. Like a marathon there are three key words here, commitment, perseverance and endurance. Some important considerations in this path are discussed below.

Physical Fitness, Mental Focus and Spirituality are the ingredients of peace

During this considerable period of reflection and mind training, I spent large amounts of my time focussing inwards. What am I thinking? Why do I think about people who irritate me even when they are not near me? Why am I thinking that? Why do I get angry? How could I be happy and suddenly become sad? Why do I think about a certain individual for a long time or repeatedly? After running a few kilometres, I realized that the chatter subsides and there is a kind of peace and happiness that steps in. The mind fascinated me since I realized that one could cry and laugh without any visible stimuli

This journey of running, reading and spirituality was motivated by my interest in the mind after the above questions occurred to me. I read extensively and kept my focus during the 5-7 hours a week running sessions. During the day, I became mindful and conscious of the need to focus on the moment and translate my learnings on a daily basis. There is no day that will go by where I would not keep this focus.

Whilst I am not making any recommendations here and it is important when you exercise you see a medical practitioner or are passed fit. The average person exercises about one and a half hours a week. I have found that to link my physical fitness to spiritual and mental success, I went beyond the norm. I exceeded the minimum amount of time spent in exercising physically which should be three hours a week. More time spent on exercises allowed me to move beyond the thoughts that result in constant chattering of the mind. In any exercise programme this happens about 25 to 30 minutes into the exercise programme.

Don't be too concerned if you gene pool is affected by certain diseases, for example, diabetes. As recent as July 2013, the New York Times published a very interesting article on exercises and its ability to change fat and muscle cells. Gretchen Reynolds argues that exercise promotes health, reducing most people's risks of developing diabetes and growing obese. What Gretchen is arguing if one is genetically predisposed, one can avoid a disease or sickness through exercise and she cites several current studies to substantiate her argument. But just how, Gretchen says, at a cellular level, exercise performs this beneficial magic—what physiological steps are involved and in what order—remains mysterious to a surprising degree. She cites several new studies that provide some clarity by showing that exercise seems able to drastically alter how genes operate.

She says genes are, of course, not static. They turn on or off; depending on what biochemical signals they receive from elsewhere in the body. When they are turned on, genes express various proteins that, in turn, prompt a range of physiological actions in the body. She articulates that one powerful means of affecting gene activity involves a process called methylation, in which methyl groups, a cluster of carbon and hydrogen atoms, attach to the outside of a gene and make it easier or harder for that gene to receive and respond to messages from the body. In this way, the behaviour of the gene is changed, but not the fundamental structure of the gene itself. Remarkably, these methylation patterns can be passed on to offspring—a phenomenon known as epigenetics.

What is particularly fascinating about the methylation process is that it seems to be driven largely by how you live your life. Many recent studies have found that diet, for instance, notably affects the methylation of genes, and scientists working in this area suspect that differing genetic methylation patterns resulting from differing diets may partly determine whether someone develops diabetes and other metabolic diseases.

But the role of physical activity in gene methylation has been poorly understood, even though exercise, like diet, greatly changes the body. So several groups of scientists recently set out to determine what working out does to the exterior of our genes. The answer, their recently published results show, is plenty according to Gretchen.

Physical exercise and the quest to find peace and be mindful cannot be separated from mental focus and spirituality. In fact all three of these are inextricable. In other words they all combine to create the conditions for peace and happiness. At a mental level, the focus has to be there continuously, each second, each minute and each day. It is a process of total dedication but this is largely influenced by your interaction with the environment. One cannot live a contradictory life. For example, one cannot hurt another person and expect to be happy or be happy when some else is grieving. One cannot create the conditions for conflict and expect peace. Almost all the readings I have done focussed me on issues of harmony and having a healthy respect for the universe which includes the environment, people and animals.

Be gentle and kind to the Universe

Spirituality embraces all living entities. For us to generate inner peace, we have to be in harmony with our surroundings. It is no coincidence that we are in the world today. There are about seven billion people and the world is approximately four billion years old. We are part of this huge universe for a reason. It is really a very beautiful place and life can be wonderful. The rivers and mountains as well as nature in general are quite remarkable. People in the majority are good and well intentioned. Our minds and background create the conditions for tension but if we are mindful of these things we can feel a lot better. There are enough resources in the world for everyone but unfortunately, there are those who want everything for themselves. Too many of the people in the world only want to receive. Giving and sharing is one definite way to find true meaning and true purpose in the world. Therefore, we need to serve humanity and treat this wonderful world with respect.

It is important to d**evelop the ability to forgive**. In most situations, it is the person who does not forgive that suffers the most. Life is temporary, we spend a short time in this universe and it is not uncommon that we find our thoughts or ideas in conflict with others. In most cases there isn't really a right and a wrong. Forgiving assists one in moving forward and shedding the baggage that forces you to live yesterday today.

Be the person that makes others feel special. It is very important to recognize the good that other people do. Try to understand why people do what they do and have compassion for people who make mistakes. By making others feel good, you feel good.

See good, do good and be good! We know that each of us have a little private mind that is shaped by our individual experiences, memory and subconscious. We are often surprised by what we think and what we say. We need to look at situations with a positive outlook. We learnt earlier that we need to accept both pleasure and pain. Life becomes far more peaceful if we are able to see the good in everything. The universe reciprocates when we do good and be good.

Love everybody. This is the most difficult practice but try learning to love people you do not appreciate or respect. It works, trust me! At worst stay away from people that you dislike. Be compassionate and work diligently on not hating the person you dislike. Hatred is more harmful to you than the other person. This will make an immense difference to your life. Negative and hostile feelings make you unhappy. Positive and loving feelings make you happy!

Service to humanity can be more important than prayer. To help a fellow human being is very important if we want to live a fulfilling life. When we acquire material things, it is very enjoyable. The challenge is that we never want to stop. Helping fellow beings who are in the margins of society provides one with a great sense of achievement. Serving the poor and less unfortunate will give you so much joy. Many people who come from poor backgrounds do not want to associate with their past when they enjoy social mobility. Recently op-ed columnist of the New York Times, Paul Krugman in the article "From mouths to Babes had this to say about what is happening in the most powerful country in the world.

.And why must food stamps be cut? We can't afford it, say politicians like Representative Stephen Fincher, a Republican of

Tennessee, who backed his position with biblical quotations—and who also, it turns out, has personally received millions in farm subsidies over the years.

Stephen says,

> look, I understand the supposed rationale: We're becoming a nation of takers, and doing stuff like feeding poor children and giving them adequate health care are just creating a culture of dependency—and that culture of dependency, not runaway bankers, somehow caused our economic crisis.

Stephen's statement has nothing to do with reality. It is his memory and sub-conscious at work here. Other people may have different views and all of them could be far from the truth. The universe should take care of its people given the abundance of resources in the world. There is enough for everybody in this world.

There is no greater satisfaction than serving humanity. I mentioned several times the concept of bad desire. I also spoke about good desire. Good desire about doing things for the greater good. We need to focus on the collective good and that will yield better dividends for all of us. If each one of us are concerned our own, the world will never be a better place.

One of our major responsibilities in the 21st century is to take care of the children throughout the world. There is no greater service one can do for the universe. Too many children are living in the margins of society. Whilst this could have been a topic for another book, I thought it was essential for me to inject this important information as it relates to good desire. It also relates to creating a better world for our children and grand-children. The architects of apartheid never thought clearly about the world they will create for their grand-children. The Nazi's never thought about the world they will create for the new generations by trying to persecute Jews. They bred hostility. Now more than ever, we need to focus on the youth, tomorrows society. It is for this reason that I have crafted the following discussion into this book.

We must create a free zone for a large percentage of children in the world given what has been elaborated on in this book about socialisation, memory and the sub-conscious on the development of people. Children have never been more neglected than they are today. From Bangladesh to Africa, including first world nations, there is just too many children that are suffering. It is a calling and the greatest gift you can give to this universe if you take care of its neglected children.

By free zone, I mean a clearer uncluttered mind. When it applies to young children of a school going age, a mind that is able to focus on reading and mathematics in the early years in schooling is a mind that is in the free zone. A mind that is cluttered with trauma, emotional pain is a mind that cannot focus on books and mathematics. Being an educationist, children have always been the focus of my attention. As a working class kid, born in an apartheid township, I had first-hand knowledge and exposure to the brutality of poverty. However, after reading and embarking on this journey, I never thought about the implications of poverty in way I do now. I have come to the realization that this world does not take care of its children. Many children because of poverty and a range of other social evils do not have the free space in their minds to grow. Their minds have too much of trauma and emotional clutter which militates against cognitive, emotional and social growth. Middle class and upper class children have different kinds of trauma which may include single parents, lack of attention and similar challenges. How does one clear the mental space for children to succeed in school and society?

It is important for all of us to think very deeply about this issue. When I visited Body Worlds which is a travelling exhibition of preserved human bodies and body parts that are prepared using a technique called plastination. I saw the human body and marvelled at its extra-ordinary perfection. What concerned me was the state of the world's children and that many of them will not be able to benefit and enjoy this human body because they are not given a chance from the time they are born. Whilst the world has enough resources for all its children, it is mainly the affluent that benefit.

The State of the World's Children 2012 report that was prepared by Unicef argues that 200 million children under 5 years of age fail to reach their full cognitive potential. Unicef also states that about 59 million children are out of school. The report indicates that many of the poor and marginalised groups live in slums and informal settlements, where they are subjected to a multitude of health risks. If we look at the slums and ghettoes Bangaladesh, South Africa, Middle East, Chicago, Harlem, and Detroit and in some place in London, we have to ask some serious questions about our humanity. We can never create the conditions of happiness if so many children grow up with so much of psychological, nutritional, educational and social damage.

What are the implications of all this? We often do not look at the psychological damage done to children from poor communities. Lack of appropriate cognitive development, fear, anxiety, lack of security, violence, alcohol, drugs and instability are the experience of many young children in the world. The perfect body I saw at Body Worlds is shaped into an inferior being by a stunted and deprived childhood. The mind, memory and sub-conscious are impacted upon in several ways. We cannot say that middle class and upper class children are untouched by trauma but they are at a distinct advantage to succeed in life. Working class and underclass children who are exposed to traumatic lives that are often impacted upon by poverty are less likely to finish school. Think about the impact that failure has on an individual, family and society. Failure reproduces failure in most instances. The spouse of a person who has failed is impacted upon. Children are brought up in this environment which is not conducive to healthy living and ultimately, the wider family and society. This environment is reproduced by new offspring and the impact is felt by many people. Therefore, governments and huge companies can make a real impact if they assist people when they are young.

I raised this issue earlier in the book where I spoke of the violence committed by adults and questioned it origin. Often the bizarre behaviour in the adult world is associated with something that went wrong in childhood. It does not have to be this way. We should all take marginalised children seriously since the world's children affects each of us. We know for every person that fails in school or fails in life, they are a potential threat to all of us. It does not matter where we live in the world. The child that fails school in South Africa could sell drugs to your children, injure you or family member and inflict injury on someone dear to you. The child in Chicago who fails in school could be involved in a mass shooting. Children who are affected by the war in Syria have a very scary future. Why does the world allow this to happen? What will the next generation of Syrian, Libyan and Iraqi children do? Any child, anywhere in the world can affect each one of us in various ways. There are a number of examples of why children should be given the best chance in life. From an economic perspective it pays for a country to invest in a child in early childhood education that invest in breaking drug cartels and paying the prison bills later in life. It is also our responsibility to take care of the children of the world since caring offers people so much of authentic joy.

The mind and how it works should be standard literature for all teachers and educationists. It should also become part of the school syllabi so that teachers and learners can develop more insight into their lives. What is the purpose of learning mathematics and science if one becomes a tyrant or a bully as an adult? How many senior people in education and the corporate have insight into themselves? Why do so many children fail in poor areas of the world? These are some of the questions that occurred to me. Life should not be this way? We need to change it and be more caring.

Don't focus on other people, focus on yourself

The greatest source of unhappiness lies in our relationships with other people. We focus on their mistakes, how they treat us and what they do to us. We often have very little control over what other people do. They are who they are because of their private minds, memories, habits and practices. We need to focus on ourselves. We need to introspect and analyse our responses. What is in us that creates this unhappiness? What weaknesses in our psyche contribute to them making us unhappy? How do we modify our responses and behaviours in relation to what they say and do to us? That will be our life long challenge. As long as we focus on others, we render ourselves weak and vulnerable. We become victims!

We spend too much of time trying to change other people. In this short time that we have in this world, we can be more constructive by changing ourselves. Being less judgemental, examining our own flaws and working on the strength of our minds and emotions. It is important to be flexible, adaptable and easy going. Life in the 21st century demands of each of us to be amenable to change and different conditions. The world around us is changing at a rapid space. Focussing on other consumes too much of valuable energy and time. Introspection and a focus on one's own mind can be the most liberating thing one can accomplish. Mahatma Gandhi said very powerfully that we should be the change we want to see.

Humour as Spiritual Practice

We are always so serious above everything and life takes its toll on us. That is why Einstein commented that he does not take himself seriously as well as others. Karen Horneffer-Ginter, in an original story in the New York Times on Jun 14, 2013, is appropriate here. It goes like this.

I was going through airport security the other month, participating in the grind of pulling out my laptop and my

Ziploc baggie full of plastic bottles, and removing my belt and my shoes and my watch and my jacket and trying to fit them all into the plastic bin in such a way that nothing would fall out as it went through its screening. On the other side, I quickly gathered my belongings so they wouldn't get run over by the oncoming stream of objects. I started shuffling forward with my shoes half on and my arms weighed down by my scattering of possessions. As I glanced up, I saw a group of chairs and tables with an accompanying sign that read: "Recombobulation Area."

Seeing the funny side of life can be far more beneficial that being frustrated if things do not go your way. The author suggests in this article there was so much relief and lightness when the sign "Recombobulation Area" was sighted. It made the whole process of the security check light and brought humour into an otherwise very stressful situation. It is important that we all find "Recombobulation Areas" when we experience the frustrations of life.

Very often we have minimal control of situations where other people make the rules. Society is highly regulated and we are forced to follow rules at most times. Therefore, it is important to see the funnier side of life or the stress has a telling effect on one over a period of time. I love watching comedians at work. They have the ability to see the funny side of life. Whilst it is a practice that is not easy to achieve if one is very serious, it is something that serious people should consider. Why be serious when each of us is wired so differently? Einstein one of our greatest thinkers offered us some important advice in this regard when he says he does not take himself or anybody else seriously. Those are wise words!

Some Final Comments

Fall Seven Times Stand Up Eight

—Japanese Proverb

Foucault said

I don't feel that it is necessary to know exactly what I am. The main interest in life and work is to become someone else that you were not in the beginning. If you knew when you began a book what you would say at the end, do you think you would have the courage to write it? What is true for writing and for a love relationship is true also for life. The game is worthwhile insofar as we don't know what will be the end.

This process of the Marathon of the Mind has left me with the thought that peace of mind is possible although I am yet to reach the finishing line. In this rapidly changing world, the complexities of life are never ending. We have to be flexible, dynamic and adaptive to what is thrown at us. This is a very long marathon with many obstacles. We cannot be naïve in believing that life has only good times. I fall on many days but I know that perseverance yields dividends. I am aware that change is possible but gradual and I am developing the ability to calm my mind gradually. Fewer things take me by surprise because I am aware of the limitations of mind and the minds of others. I know that desire is one of the biggest causes of unhappiness. When do we stop desiring is a question that persists in my mind? When will I stop wanting more?

I am conscious of my thought patterns each minute of the day. There are times when the mind gets the better of me but I am always focussing on it. I pay less attention to the negative by celebrating the positive thoughts. It has been a remarkable journey which will be on-going for the rest of my life. However, I experience more peace now than I have ever had before. When I get up in the morning my thought processes are replaced by a mantra so I know exactly what surfaces each morning in my mind. Think about the first thoughts in the morning? What do you think about? It is critical to break that pattern as it is a habit that has formed over the years. My conscious state is now more stable and I pick up immediately in many cases what causes stress. There are more occasions that I live in the now than previously. When encountering challenges, the first question I ask myself is, is this a permanent or a transient experience? How does it impact on my life and will it have an effect in next month or next year? I have stopped sweating the small stuff in the majority of instances. Whenever, a stressful thought emerges, I immediately try and source its origin. Whilst it is not always evident, I am asking the question which is important?

I have arrived at the realization that the senses can lead one astray and the mind is worse than a drunken monkey. I know when my desires are a victim of my senses and I attempt to curb this mentally. That mental intervention is enough since that reflects one is conscious of the impact of the senses. Do I need a new car? Do I need a smartphone? Should I take the lotto? Do I need a new house? Do I need this or that? Is it a want or a need? When does the endless greed for more and more stop?

During the day, I recite my personal mantra several times to shift and reduce thoughts. When something surfaces that irritates me I repeat my mantra. Regarding my belief in the Divine, it gets stronger every second and when I am discouraged a distance surfaces between the Divine and myself. I know that to get closer, I should reduce desire and surrender. This is indeed an extra-ordinary experience and I am getting stronger each day. There are times when certain incidents become alarming but that lasts for a very short period of time. Whilst I make the effort, I know that there is destiny and if something is meant to happen, it will.

The most striking advancement has been in my relationships with people. I speak less and do not believe for a moment that I have an answer for everything. The world and life is too complex for such simplicity. The one lesson I have learnt in my socialisation with others is that what I find most irritating about people is often about myself. The question I ask is what can I learn from this situation? I am able to listen and pick up more than I used to in the past. The patterns in people's behaviour, possible motivations and other characteristics are less challenging to ascertain. However, given the fact that I am aware that what I think and what they think may not be an absolute truth, my conversations and interactions are relatively peaceful. During my past I encountered many challenging experiences with people in view of my very established positions on many matters. That has subsided tremendously and has ushered a very peaceful state of mind.

It is quite an incredible experience. Trying to prove somebody wrong and examining the weaknesses of other people is now an historical thing for me. I have learnt that I should focus on my reactions and that there is really no right and wrong in this world. Everything is relative.

Most people frustrations relates to their established position on many matters. These positions that people adopt is based on the assumption that they are positing a truth. It is quite unbelievable what many people do to get their points across or try to get their ideas implemented. During my reflection, I thought that many people tried this over several centuries and endured so much of pain. There is nothing about social matters that is an absolute truth.

The biggest tragedy about advancing a position or wanting a particular view to hold or to implement a certain concept is that people will use everything at their disposal to justify it credibility and authenticity. Social experiences and social matters are in fact illusions. Based on what I have observed, it is very important that we enter every social encounter with an open mind.

The struggles of everyday life and the impact of events and people on my mental peace have reduced substantially. One of the clear conclusions that I have drawn and try to practice each day is that life is a pilgrimage and that one has to have faith, joy and steadiness each moment. At first, the idea of calming and silencing the mind may be difficult but after applying the 10 000 hour rule, it becomes easier each day. However, the focus has to be on truth, righteousness, peace and love. One has to remember that every action has a reaction. A negative thought impacts negatively and a negative deed impacts negatively.

One of the other achievements of this Marathon of Life has been my running. Through countless training sessions, I have learnt to run in a relaxed manner. Each run, each step is accompanied by a relaxed physical position and this impacts on the peace that one is attempting to create. There are less injuries and the run is far more relaxed. However, there is a long way to go and each day becomes easier but the focus has to be intense on watching the thought patterns.

The Marathon of life which involves calming the mind and creating the conditions of being happy is a life-long challenge. It DOES NOT happen overnight. Each one of us will fail at times, experience feelings of frustration but we have to stand up and keep the focus each second, each minute and each day. Try living in the present moment and do not worry about the past or the future. The moment you are upset with your progress, you are saying that all that you have achieved is wasted. Appreciate the morning air, start as early as possible living in the moment. Try breaking old habits that you do not value and that are a hindrance to your progress. It is difficult but worth it.

Of course our point of departure is that one has to have a realistic sense of happiness. The pursuit of happiness as a vague concept may result in one's unhappiness. Continuous practice of the mind will result in changes on how we think and how we respond to most situations. The key to ones' success lies in practice. I referred to Dandapani's enlightening website at the beginning of the book. I want to repeat his advice in my conclusion. His ideas on practice are worth noting.

- "Practice does not have the ability to discriminate between constructive and destructive patterns.
- "Whatever you practice is what you become good at.
- "It is a conscious choice about what you want to practice.

- "Imagine your awareness is a ball of light—As an exercise to see how this works let your mind focus your awareness on a particular thing (the last wedding you attended)—that area of your mind lights up—when it lights up that area of your mind becomes conscious.

- "Using your will power and your consciousness you can take your awareness to any area of the mind you want to—and you can hold it there for a period of time.

Remember these valuable tips on practice, each second, each minute and each day. From the first thought in the morning to the last thought when you go to bed, be conscious of what you think. Don't forget the Japanese proverb, **Fall Seven Times Stand Up Eight and practice the 10 000 hour rule**.

If you are diabetic or obese, rich or poor, if you are a smoker or a drinker, if you are depressed, if you are angry with the world, do not despair, it is your mind that can change things. A zone of peace can be achieved through exercise and you will have to translate in everyday living. Do good, be good and feel good that is the goal. Never quit. It is a great life. Don't forget to create your recombobulation area (create humour) when things get tough and don't take your life to seriously as Albert Einstein suggests but don't take other people seriously as well. Separate the temporary and transient and always ask yourself the question, does this challenge affect me in the long-term. Most challenges are temporary and after a short while it does not affect you any longer. They are all struggling to find meaning! In your toughest moments, think of Victor Frankl and how he survived! Very little can compare with that experience.

The Supreme makes everything possible that is all.